Rko 281

Jorge Consuegra

INT LARGE, DARK ROOM NIGHT

In the ebony shadows of a large room we can make out corners and edges, moldings and cornices; the phantoms of decaying Victorian wealth floating like disembodied ghosts in the darkness.

It is May 6, 1924 The harsh flare of a match being struck A shadowy male figure lights a series of nine candles on a birthday cake. Beyond the cake we can see a bed.

On the bed lies a woman in her early forties. She is ashen and sickly.

Dying.

The shadowy male figure finishes lighting the candles, blows out the match and disappears as the woman peers into the darkness.

WOMAN

Come into the light.. Come into the light

A nine-year-old boy steps into the light.

She pulls him close and whispers:

WOMAN

Never stand in the shadows --

BOY

Mother...

WOMAN

You are made for the light, Orson Now you must blow out your candles. But you must always remember, the cake itself is nothing. The flame, the lights, that is where your future lies. You must have a dream. A great dream worthy of you.

The boy immediately spins to the cake and blows out the candles. A moment of darkness. He turns back to the bed. The woman and the bed are gone, faded into darkness.

The solemn young lad stares and stares into the darkness

And then, magically, the faint glimmer of twinkling stars fill his huge dark eyes.

NEWSREEL The flickering images of an old newsreel, circa 1940 Under the MGM logo we see the title: BOY WONDER WOWS HOLLYWOOD!

The first image after the title is the imposing figure of ORSON WELLES, climbing down from an airplane and surveying the world at his feet.

Welles is 24 years old and somewhat handsome. Welles seems rather uncomfortable in his own body, as if it could not possibly contain his vast passions and appetites.

Orson Welles is man who tears his way through life with incendiary energy. He is at once inspiring and ferocious; visionary and coldly ambitious. He is part artist, part fraud and all showman.

A sonorous voice accompanies the newsreel. The voice is always grand, occasionally sardonic.

NEWSREEL VOICE

He came to the town of magic and dreams a flashing star blazing through the firmament of illusion. And he promised to devour the world in a single gulp. He was 24 years old and his name was George Orson Welles. Sound the trumpets! Unfurl the banners, Hollywood! The Boy Wonder has arrived!

Images of Welles as a baby and his early life fill the screen: Welles in a crib; as a pampered schoolboy; at dance class; drama club; dressed up for a magic show. As we hear:

NEWSREEL VOICE

He made his debut on the world stage in Kenosha, Wisconsin, on the 6th of May, 1915. And on the 7th of May he spoke his first words, and unlike other children who say commonplace things like "momma" and "poppa", he proclaimed "I am a genius!"

At three the genius was reciting Shakespeare and at eight he had taken up cigars and highballs and was learning magic from the knee of the great Houdini.

Images of Welles' early theatrical career: the young man playing impossibly old parts; vaudeville magic shows; various regional theaters; endless tawdry rehearsal rooms

Then images of Welles and JOHN HOUSEMAN in New York: the great, bustling city; Welles at work with John Houseman on a script; Welles directing a play. As we hear:

NEWSREEL VOICE

So how could the magic of the stage not call to this adventurous lad? Unstoppable and resolute, the Boy Wonder journeyed into the world of the legit theater. After a peripatetic beginning he found himself at last in New York where he joined forces with theatrical producer John Houseman under the august auspices of the WPA Federal Theater. A rehearsal room interview with John Houseman, who is in his 30's, thin-lipped and prim:

HOUSEMAN

Orson barreled in and took over. Orson's a real barreler.

Images of Welles directing his famous "Fascist JULIUS CAESAR" and "Voodoo MACBETH" productions: auditions; rehearsals; perfecting a sword-fight; rejecting classical costume sketches for JULIUS CAESAR; supervising set construction; performing Brutus in the Albert Speer- like Nuremberg rally lighting of JULIUS CAESAR. As we hear:

NEWSREEL VOICE

Like Hannibal over the Alps, the Boy Genius invaded the Great White Way. He stunned the sedate elite of New York theatre with production after production.

From MACBETH with an entirely colored cast to a Mussolini-inspired JULIUS CAESAR!

More images of New York, Welles, Houseman and radio: Welles directing a radio play with sweeping energy; supervising the elaborate sound effects; editing the script; at odds with Houseman. As we hear:

NEWSREEL VOICE

Though he wowed the critics with his spectaculars the ticket sales left something to be desired. So, after founding the Mercury Players with Houseman, young Mr. Welles quickly set his sights on the airwaves. He quickly became the sonorous -' voice of "The Shadow." "

Newsreel footage of Welles at a standing radio microphone;

WELLES
Who knows what evil lurks in the hearts of men? The Shadow knows. . .

Welles laughs his sinister Shadow laugh and we go to more images of radio and the dynamic Welles performing and directing as we hear:

NEWSREEL VOICE
With Lament Cranston in one pocket and his own radio show. The Mercury Theater of the Air, our Boy Wonder filled the night with his resounding tones.

And on October 30th of 1938, he became what he felt destined to be: a household name. What started out as a roguish Halloween prank became the most famous radio show in the history of the galaxy!

Images of the WAR OF THE WORLDS broadcast and panic: listeners huddling next to their radios; telephone switchboards lighting up; New Jersey State Motorcycle Troopers zooming down rural roads; cars clogging the highways. As we hear:

NEWSREEL VOICE
THE WAR OF THE WORLDS sent this nation spinning into a frenzy. Nine million listeners clasped their loved ones close and looked to the skies with horror. Unlucky listeners near the epicenter of the "invasion" -- rural New Jersey -- ran screaming into the night, sure a monstrous alien and a fiery death awaited them around every corner! The mischievous Boy Wonder had fooled us all!

Newsreel footage of a packed press conference with Welles the day following the broadcast:

WELLES
(contritely)
Of course ... of course ... if I had known the panic the broadcast was causing -- well I would have stopped! I never meant for any of this to happen and I feel just horrible!

Quick newsreel clips of Welles leaving the press conference with Houseman. We see them slip into a taxi. Inside the taxi we can just glimpse Welles exploding with laughter.

NEWSREEL VOICE
How long, oh how long could it possibly be before the sunny land of dreams tried to harness the combustible power of this showman, this impresario, this best of all possible Boy Wonders?!

Images of Welles posing and shaking hands with GEORGE

SCHAEFER
Schaefer is an intense, compact man in his early 50's. His nickname in

Hollywood is "The Tiger" -- both for his admired tenacity and his feared temper. He is a moral and ethical man; John Adams in a Brooks Brothers suit.
As we hear

NEWSREEL VOICE
The winner in the Welles derby was George Schaefer, the head of RKO Pictures. With a contract unimaginable before The Days Of Orson, Mr. Schaefer captured the whirlwind snared the beast, roped the tyrant!
Images of Welles and Schaefer: Welles signing his contract; smiling to Schaefer; Schaefer making a speech; Welles joking with reporters. As we hear:

NEWSREEL VOICE
Eyebrows raised and jaws dropped all over Hollywoodland when the terms of the deal that lured The Great Orson came forth: the Boy Wonder could produce, write, direct and star in his own projects with budgets up to $500,000 a picture! He would have total control over the shooting of the picture and the finished product. The studio, well, they just paid the bills. Meanwhile, the insiders of filmland were skeptical. An interview with a Hollywood Insider, who looks like a bookie:

HOLLYWOOD INSIDER
John Ford doesn't have a deal like that. Cecil B.
DeMille doesn't have a deal like that. No one has a deal like that! If ya ask me, George Schaefer is just plain nuts Images of Welles arriving in Hollywood and touring the town: Welles climbing down from a plane; posing with Schaefer before of the RKO gates; touring the studio; leaning over an editing machine; laughing with female extras in the commissary; posing in front of his Brentwood home. As we hear:

NEWSREEL VOICE
So Cometh Orson! He toured the RKO studio and met with the biggest of the big! He charmed his way through the town from the Brown Derby to the
Copacabana, from the Pacific Palisades to the Hollywood Hills!
More images of Welles in Hollywood: Welles touring the town; visiting all the nightclubs and dancing with beautiful women; he is seen everywhere about the town. As we hear:

NEWSREEL VOICE
Yes, the Boy Wonder had arrived! He even charmed those rival maidens of Hollywood gossip, those well- coiffured chroniclers of the dream factory: Hedda
Hopper and Louella Parsons.
Shots of Welles with LOUELLA PARSONS and HEDDA HOPPER
Louella is a much-feared gossip columnist. She is a gorgon in her 60's;
Margaret Dumont possessed by the devil and tanked up on gin. Her capricious cruelty is only matched by her fervent loyalty to all things
Hearstian.

Hedda is a gossip columnist in her 50's. She is given to elaborate hats and villainous intrigue. Louella's younger, smarter rival, Hedda probably spends her spare time eating children.

Then a snippet of an interview with Louella:

LOUELLA
Orson is the sweetest boy. We're both from the midwest, you know. He's just a local fella making good, ya follow?

More shots of Welles just after his arrival in Hollywood, blissfully touring the RKO facilities as:

NEWSREEL VOICE
So today, almost a year after his arrival in
Hollywood, we leave the Boy Wonder still hard at work developing his much-anticipated first feature, preparing to dazzle us all again. We're waiting,
Orson!

Welles after his RKO tour, smiling mischievously, stands before a microphone:

WELLES
I'll tell you what, this is the best electric train set a boy ever had!

"The End" and newsreel credits

The newsreel sputters to a stop in a screening room. A shaft of light shines on a large MGM logo on one wall. Another shaft of light illuminates the sitting figure of LOUIS B. MAYER.

Mayer is a short, crafty, bespectacled man in his 50's. His cloying, avuncular exterior only fleetingly disguises the film titan's outrageous barbarism.

Another shadowy figure, a Mayer FLUNKIE, can be just glimpsed sitting elsewhere in the screening room.

Mayer glowers at the darkened screen for a moment.

A beat.

MAYER
Who does that cocksucker think he is?

FLUNKIE
They're laying bets over on the RKO lot that this great deal will end up with him never doing a picture. Back to New York he goes.

MAYER
Serves him right. I mean can you stomach the arrogance?

FLUNKIE
Inside skinny says the glory boy's finished, can't come up with a movie. Wants to do a biography now.

MAYER

After RKO boots him maybe we'll pick him up cheap.
Have him do that WAR OF THE WORLDS crap as a feature.
Meantime, shelve the newsreel. No one cares

INT SAN SIMEON. WELLES' SUITE EVENING
Orson Welles, elegant and impressive, is flourishing a cigarette and a coin in his magnificently expressive hands He is perfecting a magic trick.
Welles is lounging on the bed of an enormous guest suite at San Simeon.
He is wearing a tuxedo.
In the bathroom beyond him we can see the writer HERMAN MANKIEWICZ

("MANK".)
Mank is a wonderful wreck of a human being. 43 years old, but looking considerably older, he is short and squat and bitter. A compulsive gambler and drinker, Mank still glimmers with wry humor that is equally wicked and corrosive. He is incomplete without the stub of a cigar clenched in his teeth.
Mank, also dressed in a tuxedo, is looking at himself in the bathroom mirror as he struggles with his bow tie. He occasionally glances in the mirror to Welles.
Title: JANUARY 3, 1940

MANK

I don't know what you expected with Joseph- fucking-Conrad for Chrissake. I mean this
is
Hollywood, pal.

WELLES

All right! Enough! I've heard this from Schaefer and RKO. I've heard it from everyone-
-

MANK

But you keep coming up with the same elitist crap -
- HEART OF DARKNESS with a million dollar budget?! -
- no one wants to see that.

WELLES
Nonsense
Welles dramatically taps the cigarette on the coin, practicing his trick as:

MANK
What are movies about, Orson?

WELLES
Forget it-

MANK
What are movies about?

WELLES
Telling stories.

MANK
Nope.

WELLES
Showing life

MANK
Who the hell wants to see life?! People are sick to death of life! They want make-believe, pal. Fantasy.
They want Tarzan and Jane, not Tristan and Isolde.
Welles quickly makes the cigarette seem to completely pass through the coin. An astounding bit of slight of hand.

WELLES
(happily)
Magic

MANK
Butts on seats. That's what movies are about. You got one job in Hollywood -- everyone has the same job, in fact -- putting the butts on the seats. You gotta sell 'em popcorn and Pepsi- cola. It's all about popcorn and Pepsi-cola.

WELLES
Not for me.

MANK
Then you better get ready to be the youngest never- was in Hollywood history.

WELLES
That's better than being the oldest has-been in
Hollywood history.

MANK
You're a laugh-riot, kid.
Welles laughs and goes to Mank in the bathroom.

WELLES
Here, turn around.
Welles ties Mank's bow tie for him as:

WELLES
So, we've got to come up with our movie. Our biography.

MANK
Right-

WELLES
We find the man and then we dissect him-

MANK
Like a bug.

WELLES
But with compassion and insight--

MANK
(glancing at his watch)
Christ, we gotta go! The old man doesn't cotton to lateness.
Mank takes a quick swig from a flask of vodka, shoves it into his coat and scurries into
the other room as Welles checks himself in the mirror.
A beat. Welles smiles, confident and resplendent

WELLES
(into the mirror)
How do you do, Mr. Hearst? My name is Orson
Welles.

INT SAN SIMEON. HALLWAY FOLLOWING
Welles and Mank walk through an impressive upstairs hallway of San
Simeon. Quick glimpses of the astounding grandeur everywhere around them as:

WELLES
How about Howard Hughes? We could do Hughes

MANK
I'm not fucking with Hughes. That shit-kicker would kill us dead, baby. Just like Jean
Harlow

WELLES
Howard Hughes killed Jean Harlow?

MANK
Sure. Dropped her out of his Lockheed over Utah
They disappear down a long stairway

INT SAN SIMEON. DINING HALL EVENING
An explosion of color and an immediate swirl of sound
We are in the Grand Refectory -- the mammoth dining room -- at San

Simeon. Five long tables are placed end to end. There are about fifty sumptuously dressed guests.

WILLIAM RANDOLPH HEARST and MARION DAVIES preside, side by side, at the center table.

Hearst is 76 years old. He is a fully commanding figure, towering in both height (six foot two) and personality. He is shaped rather like a pear and moves with a delicacy surprising for such a famously merciless man. Although the word ruthless does not begin to do justice to the press baron's animus, Hearst is endlessly polite and almost painfully soft-spoken.

Marion is 43 years old, a shimmering and lively presence. In a word that might have been coined for her, she has moxie. While the ravages of alcoholism have left their subtle marks on the edges and attitudes of her face, she can still charm and captivate with almost effortless grace.

Around Hearst's feet sit a collection of his beloved dachshunds.

On the other side of the main table, and down a bit, sit Welles and Mank.

We sweep around the table, hearing bits of overlapping dialogue and finally settle on Marion and Hearst.

Marion is charming CAROLE LOMBARD and CLARK GABLE, who sit beside her. She tenderly rests one hand on Hearst's arm as she speaks. Marion speaks with an occasionally pronounced stutter.

MARION

And we would hear them scuttling around at night with their little red eyes and little yellow t-t- teeth and I'm just imagining plague lice jumpin' all over the damn place So we set t-t-traps everywhere.

And every morning we would find the t-t-traps sprung but no mice!

CAROLE LOMBARD

Houdini mice.

Laughter

MARION

Just wait. So one night I notice Pops getting outta bed and sneaking away. And he's got this little p-p- paper bag with him, right? Middle of the night. So I figure the old man's really up to no good this time and I follow him. Well I'll be g-g-goddamned if he's not springing all the traps and leaving cheese for the rats!

MARION

You and that freak Disney, in love with the damn rats!

Laughter, even from Hearst

HEARST

They really are sweet little things

Meanwhile, across the table Welles is rapaciously devouring his dinner as:

WELLES
Sigmund Freud?

MANK
Kid, you just got your ass kicked on Joseph Conrad and now you're gonna go to Schaefer
and tell him you wanna do the id and the superego? Stop being so goddamn smart.
Mank surreptitiously pours a huge shot of vodka from his flask into his glass as:

WELLES
(suddenly inspired)
Manolete?!

MANK
Who the hell's Manolete?

WELLES
The great Spanish bullfighter

MANK
I don't wanna write about no spic.

WELLES
No, it's perfect! When in doubt, put on a cape!
False noses and faux beards and flowing capes have been the life-blood of the actor's
craft since the days of Irving and Booth. (He flourishes his napkin like a bullfighter's
cape.) Imagine me in a glittering suit of lights on the dusky Andalusian plains--

MARION
Why Mr. Welles is attempting semaphore
Welles smiles across the table.
Laughter.

WELLES
Bullfighting, Miss Davies!

MARION
And is dear Mank your b-b-bull?

WELLES
My factotum, ally and comrade-in-arms

MANK
Writer, flunkie, pimp--

CAROLE LOMBARD
(wry)

You fight many bulls there in New York, Orson?

WELLES
Ever met Walter Winchell?

WELLES
(expansively, warming into a story)
No, when I was but a tender lad--

CAROLE LOMBARD
Last week would this be?
Laughter. As Welles speaks the whole table gradually stops eating and listens to his tale:

WELLES
My father and I made a tour of the grand boulevards of antique Europe. And when we were in Iberia I had the chance to face the bulls. At the knee of the great Manolete I took up the cape and sword -
(he uses his napkin and knife to demonstrate)
-- across from me stood a mammoth bull reputed to have gored a full seven men to a grisly demise! So -
- with Manolete shouting encouragement I flourished
...I flourished again ...and the bull charged!
Across the golden dust it came, thundering like the great minotaur of legend, closer, ever closer, its calamitous hooves pounding into the dirt, shaking the earth as I held the crimson eye of the bull with my own, defying it -- it was almost upon me and I flourished one last time! -- the monster swept past!

-
(he spins his napkin in the air and his knife is now gone, a magic trick)
-- and my sword was gone -- buried in the bloody eye of the beast!
Applause and laughter from around the table. Then:

HEARST
(quietly)
You are evidently a man who knows a great deal about bull.
Some nervous titters. A beat as Welles' smile fades and he stares at Hearst.

HEARST
Of all man's malignity -- of all his sadism -- none is more depraved than cruelty to animals.
Silence
Mank gives Welles a desperate warning look to keep quiet Welles cannot resist speaking:

WELLES
In Spain the cruelty would be in denying the beast a fighting end.
A beat as Hearst rivets Welles with a cold, bland stare Deafening silence around the
table.
Then:

HEARST
Who are you, sir?

WELLES
My name is Orson Welles

HEARST
The actor

WELLES
And director.

HEARST
I see. And you are in California for what reason?

WELLES
To make pictures.

HEARST
And what pictures have you made?
A beat.

WELLES
None.
A beat. Hearst smiles

HEARST
Well, I wish you luck. It is a treacherous business.

WELLES
So I've been told.

HEARST
In Hollywood the fiercest bulls are the most brutally killed.

WELLES
I'll remember that.
A tense beat. Marion quickly diffuses the situation;

MARION

Enough Hollywood talk! Can't anyone talk about anything else?

MANX
Heard some juicy gossip from Metro.

MARION
(eagerly)
Ooh, dish.
Laughter. Even from Hearst. Then the dinner chatter continues.
Welles cannot keep his eyes off Hearst, the press baron draws Welles in like a siren.
Marion gives Hearst a little kiss and grabs Carole Lombard and they leave the table.
Hearst leans into Clark Gable to continue talking.
Welles sits back and reaches for a cigar. Mank takes his arm and indicates he should stop, nodding his head in Hearst's direction.

WELLES
(quietly)
The man doesn't allow drinking or cigars? This is monstrous.

MANK
The old man has his own way of doing things

WELLES
He's nothing but a hypocrite. He preaches morality every day in his sordid little papers for everyone else in the world but he lives openly with his mistress.
Mank sneaks another shot from his flask

MANK
Buddy, when you own the largest publishing empire in the universe you can do whatever the hell you want. Think about it, pal. Every day one out of five
Americans picks up a Hearst publication. 30 newspapers, a dozen magazines, a bunch of radio stations and the grand dragon of them all. Little
Miss Louella Parsons. Tends to give you some of that ol' noblesse oblige.
Welles studies Hearst across the table.

WELLES
Look at those hands. Those are the hands of an artist. A modern Caravaggio.

MANK
No, baby, those are the hands of a killer
Hearst leans down and feeds his favorite pet dachshund, Helen, table scraps. He talks to her gently.

HEARST
There you are, honey. Aren't you a wonderful girl?

INT SAN SIMEON. LADIES LOUNGE FOLLOWING
Marion and Carole Lombard escape into an ornate ladies bathroom.
Marion immediately goes to a cabinet and retrieves a bottle of Scotch hidden under some towels. She takes a swig and then hands the bottle to
Carole Lombard. She drinks.
Marion lights a cigarette.

MARION
God, these parties are the worst

CAROLE LOMBARD
You need to get outta here, Rapunzel

MARION
That's why he has the parties, he says it's like bringing the world to me.

CAROLE LOMBARD
Why don't you come down to LA? Stay with us for a while.

MARION
With about twenty of his spies on my tail. No thanks.
Marion hands the cigarette to Carole Lombard A beat.
A beat.

MARION
(somewhat ruefully)
It's not so bad here. After all, what girl doesn't want to live in a castle?

MARION
Mr. Welles certainly is a caution

CAROLE LOMBARD
(smiles)
Yeah, Orson's a real piece of work. But deep down, he's a good kid. Real deep down.

MARION
And attractive in a hammy sort of way.

CAROLE LOMBARD
Mm.
A beat. Carole Lombard hands the cigarette back to Marion

CAROLE LOMBARD
Listen, you come down and stay with us for a few days. Just tell the old man that--

MARION

I can't

CAROLE LOMBARD
Sure you can, just--

MARION
He needs me here.
A beat. Carole Lombard does not respond.

INT SAN SIMEON. BALLROOM FOLLOWING
In the cavernous ballroom, a dance band is playing "I'LL BE SEEING

YOU."
The guests mingle and dance
Welles and Mank wander as Welles takes in the impressive surroundings.

WELLES
"In Xanadu did Kubla Khan a stately pleasure dome decree..."How big is it, all told?
The estate?

MANK
The whole joint is half the size of Rhode Island.

WELLES
Jesus

MANK
Yeah, it's the place God would have built, if he'd had the money.
Carole Lombard and Marion return, rather giggly

MARION
Mankie, Mankie d-d-dance with me

MANK
You've been naughty, haven't you, honey?

MARION
Shit, can you smell it? You got any sen-sen?

MANK
Sorry.

MARION
Mr. Welles, you got any--? Oh fuck it.
She goes off in search of Hearst.

CAROLE LOMBARD
Meanwhile, Orson, I thought your bullfighting story was nifty. Let's cut a rug.
She pulls Welles to the dance floor Mank wanders away and takes another swig from
his flask.
As Welles and Carole Lombard dance, Welles keeps an eye on Hearst and
Marion who are dancing nearby.

CAROLE LOMBARD
So you ever gonna do a picture?

WELLES
Not you too

CAROLE LOMBARD
(smiles)
It's gonna be fine, Orson. You're gonna do great.

WELLES
I wonder sometimes.

CAROLE LOMBARD
You're just scared.

WELLES
Am I?

CAROLS LOMBARD
Sure

WELLES
And what am I scared of?

CAROLE LOMBARD
Of being found out. Of not being a genius

WELLES
(smiles)
Oh, but haven't you heard? I'm the Boy Wonder.
I've been a genius since the moment I was born.

CAROLE LOMBARD
We've known each other too long, Orson. Sling the bullshit elsewhere.

WELLES
Carole, you wound me! As if I could hope to pacify you with evasions of--

CAROLE LOMBARD
Don't insult me with your cute press quotes Save it for Louella.
She stops and looks at him firmly

CAROLE LOMBARD
You make your mark, Orson.
Nearby Marion pulls away from Hearst sharply, drawing Welles' attention. He overhears:

MARION
Goddamn it. I gotta have some kinda life!

HEARST
There's no call for that language-

MARION
There certainly is I There certainly is! Aw, to hell with you!
She storms off. Welles and Carole Lombard watch her go

WELLES
That poor woman.

CAROLE LOMBARD
(sadly)
She knew what she was signing on for After all, she took the money.
Welles watches as Hearst stands alone on the dance floor We hear the sound of a lion roaring in the distance

INT SAN SIMEON. WELLES' SUITE NIGHT
Welles, again dressed in a tuxedo, lies on his bed
Through the open balcony doors he can hear the eerie sound of lions roaring and elephants trumpeting in the night.
He stand and wanders to the balcony. Below him he can see bits and pieces of Hearst's private zoo in the moonlight: a lion pacing relentlessly back and forth; an alligator slipping into the water; a monkey slamming into the bars of its cage.
The disquieting sounds of the menagerie float through the midnight air.
Welles leaves his suite

INT SAN SIMEON. HALLWAYS FOLLOWING
Welles roams the seemingly endless hallways of San Simeon. In the half- light they begin to resemble his own cinematic dream-palace, Xanadu.
He hears the ghostly echo of a song, "WHERE OR WHEN".
He curiously follows the sound, taking in the fabulous castle everywhere around him.
He passes by the door to the Assembly Room. Inside, shafts of light illuminate portions of huge, uncompleted jigsaw puzzles.

INT SAN SIMEON. BALLROOM FOLLOWING
"WHERE OR WHEN" is now clear.
Welles stands in the shadows of a balcony overlooking the great ballroom.
Below him a phonograph record spins lazily on a turntable standing of the floor of the deserted ballroom.
And Hearst and Marion are enjoying a quiet dance together, her head nestled on his shoulder.
Welles stares and stares at them And slowly smiles. We linger on Hearst and Marion as they dance

EXT WELLES' HOUSE. POOL DAY
Welles, wrapped in a bathrobe, is pacing quickly around the perimeter of his backyard pool. He is puffing on a cigar and grunting to himself as he scribbles down notes.
Mank, wearing sunglasses and a battered fedora and looking decidedly hung-over, comes from the house to the pool.
Welles roars up to him:

WELLES
Mank! You scoundrel! What took you so long?!

MANK
(pained)
Orson, please ... it's too bright
Welles takes Mank's fedora and flings it away.

WELLES
Here you are, up with the birds for once, you vampire!

MANK
(settling into a deck chair)
Okay, boy wonder, what?

WELLES
Listen ... I've got it! It came to me like a thief in the night! Pure inspiration! Total magnificence!
Mank takes a glass from a tray of orange juice and pours vodka from a flask into his juice as:

MANK
Oh for Christ's sake-

WELLES
I know who we're going to get I The great American biography! A journey into the soul of the beast.

MANK

This better be good

WELLES
Image a man that has shaped his time. A titanic figure of limitless influence. Think about empire. A man with an empire at his feet. A man, like a baron, living in a palace, a glorious palace on a hill, and controlling the permutations of everyone beneath him. Feudal.

MANK
(realizing)
Oh Christ...

WELLES
Image the possibilities as this man controls the public perception of the nation through his--

MANK
Oh Christ
A beat as Welles stands in triumph before Mank.

WELLES
Yes.

MANK
(quietly)
Please don't say this.

WELLES
Mank-

MANK
Don't whisper it. Don't even think it

WELLES
How long have we spent casting our minds about the world when the answer to our prayers was right here under our noses -- every single day in the newspapers and on the radio -- waiting for us in that ridiculous castle! Waiting for--!

MANK
Orson. Stop. Just stop
Welles quickly sits in a deck chair next to Mank as:
Beat

WELLES
Now remember he's a public figure who sought out that publicity so legally he can't stop us from--

MANK
(laughs coldly) Listen to you. You child! Men like him don't bother with things like
legality. They don't have to.
You know why, boy-o? Power. Power like you couldn't even begin to imagine.

MANK
Howard Hughes, he would just kill us. Hearst he would kill us and fuck everything we
ever loved.

WELLES
We're doing Hearst.
A beat. Mank slowly removes his sunglasses and leans forward, dead serious.
A beat.

MANK
You may think you know what you're talking about, kid, but believe me, you don't.
You're talking about going into a battle you can never win on a battlefield so far above
things like movies and
Hollywood that Hearst won't even have to glance down when he crushes you. When he
flicks you away with one finger. I'm talking about money and influence and evil beyond
your capacity to imagine Hell.

WELLES
So speaks the court jester.

MANK
Fuck you

WELLES
I expected more from you.

MANK
Sorry to disappoint.

WELLES
(with building venom)
How does it feel, Mank? Going up to the palace and making all the lords and ladies
laugh as you tell your little stories and beg for crumbs at the table?
How does it feel being the ugly little monkey they keep to amuse themselves--?!
Mank leaps to his feet

MANK
It feels just fine, you pompous fuck-
Welles blocks Mank's way. Mank retreats. Welles pursues him around the pool as:

WELLES

I remember a man who wrote I He was a brilliant writer who dazzled me time and time again with his wit and insight--

MANK

Don't do this

WELLES

Where did he go? He hasn't had a screen credit in four years--

MANK

Don't do this

WELLES

(savagely)

--Because he has been so furiously busy wasting himself. Amusing his keepers. Because he is a sycophant! Because he has been thrown out of every studio in Hollywood and no one will hire him because he's a drunk- -!

Mank spins on him:

MANK

AND YOU'RE NOTHING BUT A GODDAMN PHONY! What is all this "Orson Welles" bullshit?! This boy genius crap?! What the fuck did you ever CREATE? You're just another goddamn ACTOR!

Welles shoves Mank violently. Mank goes sailing into the pool.

Mank splashes to the surface and stands for a shocked moment and then wades to the edge of the pool. Miraculously, and like the true drinker he is, Mank is still holding his glass of juice and vodka, now supplemented with pool water.

Welles stands above him, blocking his exit from the pool. From this low angle Welles suddenly looks startlingly Kane- like.

A pause

MANK

Let me out.

WELLES

Listen to me-

MANK

Fuck you--

WELLES

I am giving you the last chance you will ever have to be yourself again!

MANK

(suddenly)

I don't have it anymore?!

MANK
When I was a kid I wanted to scorch the world too -
- I had all kinda dreams about making great pictures and telling great stories. But all
that's finished for me--

WELLES
It doesn't have to be

MANK
And yeah, sure, Hearst's a great subject. Been keeping notes on him for years for my ...
(he laughs bitterly) great American novel. But I can't do it anymore. No studio's gonna
hire me and I - -

WELLES
I'll hire you -- right now-

MANK
I can't do it. okay?! I drink too much -- I drink all the fucking time and I don't have it
anymore.
All that is over for me--

WELLES
(roars)

NOT UNLESS I. TELL YOU IT IS
A tense pause
Welles kneels by the edge of the pool, effortlessly switching gears.

WELLES
(deeply)
Look, Mank, this is our only chance
I know this is the story. And now is the time. And I cannot do it without you. Everything
in my life -- all the promise and potential and dreams -- have led to this moment right
now. To you and me. Right here.
A pause. Welles gazes at Mank, imploring

MANK
He'll destroy us.

WELLES
Then let him. What have we got to lose, you and I?
A long beat Welles leans close to him.

WELLES

Take my hand, Mank. And we'll dance one last time.
We'll dance to the music of the angels. We'll make history. We'll scorch the earth. We will ... astonish them all.
Silence as Welles offers his hand to Mank.
Mank takes a sip from his glass of juice, vodka and pool water.

MANK
Thank God you don't write dialogue

INT WELLES' LIVING ROOM DAY
Mank is slowly sharpening a series of pencils with a pocket knife, blank pads waiting.
Welles is standing across the room from him.

WELLES
So, who is he? We have to know him.

MANK
Everyone sees someone different. That's what we show.

WELLES
How?

MANK
Like a jewel. Turn it in the light and a different facet is illuminated.
Mank finishes sharpening his last pencil and picks up a pad He smiles to Welles

MANK
Go
And we leap into MONTAGE -- WELLES AND MANK BRAINSTORM
A rush of jazzy. Gene Krupa percussion as Welles and Mank develop their story.
We see images of feverish creativity. Welles raging, pleading, arguing, pushing. Mank responding, laughing, drinking, writing.
It is a passionate dance of creation Welles' tennis court Mank and
Welles are on the tennis court, but hard at work.
Mank waits for Welles to serve. Welles bounces the tennis ball, but is too preoccupied to serve as:

WELLES
The key -- the key -- the clue -- what does this man recall on his death bed? Okay, Mank, you're dying. What's the last image that comes to you?
Right now.

MANK
This girl on a dock. White dress. Never said a word to her.

WELLES

Why her?

MANK
She was ...innocent
A beat, Welles deep in thought. Mank watches Welles closely.

MANK
So when was our man innocent? Was there a moment early on -- of innocence and bliss?
There must have been. Okay, you're dying - what do you think?
Welles does not answer. He continues to bounce the tennis ball, deep in thought.
A beat

MANK
(probing)
Something you lost maybe?

MANK
Something you can never get back?
Mank watches as Welles lets the tennis ball drop. It bounces and rolls
-- for a fleeting moment in Welles' mind it seems to become the rolling snow globe from
KANE -- we hear the sound of sleigh bells and a child's happy voice -- in the snow
globe we seem to see a boy laughing and pelting his father with snowballs. . .
Then more images, mad and outlandish and sedate and solemn; in the kitchen, in a car,
around the pool, in a bar.
Welles and Mank act out scenes and argue. They leap from character to character
fearlessly. Emoting and laughing and writing. We see the twin joy and terror of walking
the tightrope, of sheer creation.
We see them having a ferocious argument. They scream back and forth angrily and then
Mank storms out and slams the door. Welles stands alone in his living room, he catches
a glimpse of his own reflection in a mirror and we hear:

MANK'S VOICE
Men like Hearst don't love..
Welles' living room: Welles is slowly advancing on Mank.
Mank sits, watching Welles approach. The living room is now filthy.
Papers and sketches and gin bottles are discarded everywhere around them, a thick
cloud of cigar smoke. It is very late at night and the room is in semi-darkness.

WELLES
All men love. But men like Hearst -- they don't bother with convention because--

MANK
They don't have to.

WELLES

He loves in his own way. On his conditions. Because those are the only conditions he has ever known.

Welles is now standing over Mank, a dark figure in silhouette. Mank soaks in this somewhat ominous image.

More music and images: eating and working; swimming and working; playing and working simultaneously.

Then: Beach:

Sunset. We see them walking along a deserted beach Welles is walking in the surf, his trousers rolled.

WELLES
(quietly)
Hearst looks down at the world at his feet
Everything has always been beneath him.

MANK
And what does he see?

WELLES
The people. When they pay him homage, he adores them. But when they have the ... audacity to question him. To doubt him. To embarrass him. Then he despises them.

MANK
And when he looks up? What does he dream about?

31
Welles stops and looks up. A thousand stars twinkle above him. They are reflected in his eyes.
A long pause as he does not answer Mank Then

MANK
I'm ready to write it, Orson
Welles turns to him. You're sure?
Yeah. Mank gazes at Welles.

WELLES
MANK
I know him The clatter of an old typewriter is heard. EXT/INT +

BUNGALOW. VICTORVILLE DAY
Victorville is a rural desert community in San Bernadino County about
90 miles from LA.
Mank and John Houseman are ensconced in a bungalow at Campbell's Guest
Ranch, writing the movie.

Mank, smoking a cigar, paces around the cacti and shrubs in the backyard reciting to their secretary. She pounds away on a typewriter as he orates. A huge stack of papers lies neatly by her typewriter.
This is clearly the longest screenplay in the history of the world.

MANK
Leiand: "You talk about the people as if you owned them. As though they belonged to you. But you don't really care about anything except you." Craig: "A toast then, Jedediah, to all those people who didn't vote for me today and to love on my own terms. Those are the only terms anybody ever knows..."
We float into the house as we continue to hear Mank's recitation...
Inside, John Houseman is busy rifling through Mank's room as he listens:

MANK'S VOICE (CONT.)
"...because in the end a man looks into the mirror and sees one face looking back not humanity -- not
"the people" -- one face. And he's got to be able to look at that one face and know he was true. "
Houseman uncovers a bottle of vodka hidden under Mank's bed He pours the bottle down a bathroom drain as he calls out the window:

JOHN HOUSEMAN
That's too long. Tighten it up
Outside, Mank snarls and then revises:

MANK
You're killin' me here, Housey. Okay, make that,
Craig: "A toast, Jedediah, to love on my own terms.
Those are the only terms anybody ever knows, his own."
Houseman emerges from the house.

JOHN HOUSEMAN
Telegram from The Christ Child
He tears open the telegram and reads:
Beat.

JOHN HOUSEMAN
"Schaefer loves the idea. Stop. Start writing.
Stop. Stop drinking. Stop. Did you work in the jigsaw puzzles. Question mark. Don't stop. Stop.
Love you madly, Orson."

MANK
That man makes my brain hurt
We fade to a beautiful drawing of a dark, cavernous room. Perhaps it is a perfect matte painting from KANE. Real or illusion? The image turns into...

INT SOUND STAGE, RKO LOT DAY
Welles is standing in the middle of an enormous sound stage, empty but for a table with some elaborate set models. He is;' slowly walking around the models, studying them, imagining' his movie.
The sound stage door opens and a man enters, carrying a small black bag. He is cinematographer GREGG TOLAND.
Toland is a quiet, efficient and slim man of 36. He is brilliant and fearless.
Toland walks to Welles and, without a word, pulls an Oscar statue out of the bag and sets it down in the middle of one of the set models. He looks up at Welles as we hear:

WELLES' VOICE
And Gregg Toland plunks down his Oscar for
WUTHERING HEIGHTS and says, "Mr. Welles, I want to shoot your picture..."

INT THE BROWN DERBY DAY\NIGHT
The chic Brown Derby restaurant is the unquestioned palace of Hollywood celebrities. The smug big-wigs and desperate hangers-on circulate and score points in the Great Game of Movie Gossip.
In one corner booth sits Hedda Hopper, phoning in the latest salacious gossip to her newspaper. In the other corner booth Louella Parsons does the same. They occasionally glance back and forth at each other like ravenous hyenas eyeing the last bit of carrion.
Welles circulates between them. In a scene reminiscent of the famous
CITIZEN KANE breakfast table scene with Kane and Emily, we shoot back and forth as Welles applies his considerable charm to both women.
Welles is dressed differently with each of them; breakfast with Hedda and dinner with Louella.
With Hedda, morning:

WELLES (CONT.)
... And I said, "Mr. Toland, you are the finest cinematographer in Hollywood, why would you desire to work with a stumbling neophyte?"
With Louella, night

WELLES
And he replied, "Mr. Welles, the only way to learn anything new is to work with someone who doesn't know a damn thing."
Louella screeches

LOUELLA
(scribbling on a pad)
Priceless!
With Hedda, morning:

WELLES
Hedda, this movie is going to look like no other picture ever made.

With Louella, night:

WELLES
Tome it's a question of truth and illusion. Don't you get tired of the errant falsity in motion pictures?

LOUELLA
Huh?

WELLES
What we are going to do is shoot life -- in all it's joyous complexity.
He takes out a coin and begins a magic trick

WELLES
Consider this quarter, my dear. You can touch it and feel it and were you to lean forward you could even smell it. Why is it that in the movies a simple bit of reality -- a quarter, a room, a man--
With Hedda, morning:

WELLES
Becomes nothing but a lie? A trick. An illusion.
He makes the quarter 'completely disappear. Hedda is charmed

WELLES
I will show the reality behind the trick.
He makes the quarter appear again and shows the guts of the trick.

WELLES
I will use the illusions of Hollywood to show ...the truth.

HEDDA
What does truth have to do with movies?
With Louella, night

LOUELLA
(confused)
So, what, it went into your other hand?
With Hedda, morning:

WELLES
And so the dreamer awakens into the realms of reality. He has been given a rendition of the truth.
He has been treated with respect.

HEDDA

Orson, that's all terribly interesting but what's all this about you and Dolores Del Rio?
Do I hear love birds a'singin'?
Welles sighs. With Louella, night:

LOUELLA
Now, Orson, you know I'm just dyin' to see your picture and I know it's gonna be boffo,
but you're writing about a publisher, right?

WELLES
We're using-

LOUELLA
You're not doin' Hearst, are you?

WELLES
Good God no! The character is a delicious amalgamation of various press barons--

LOUELLA
A delicious amalgamation, is it?
He leans forward to light her cigarette as:

WELLES
That's right. A symphony of those: vaunted and valued tellers-of-truth. Those heroic
minutemen standing sentry on our liberties--

EXT.
LOUELLA
Orson, hold on. Look into my eyes. Tell me you are not doing Hearst.

WELLES
I am not doing Hearst.

INT BUNGALOW. VICTORVILLE DAY
Mank and Houseman watch nervously as Welles reads the last page of their massive
screenplay.
The script, almost half a foot high, is piled on a table next to
Welles.
He sets down the last page and looks at Mank. A beat

WELLES
It's 350 pages long.

MANK
Yeah, but the margins are real wide.

WELLES

It is 350 pages of ... ABSOLUTE INSPIRATION!
He leaps up and embraces Mank

WELLES
Housey, get us a drink.
Houseman glances at Welles, surprised, but dutifully scampers inside.

WELLES
I told you you could do this! How could you have ever doubted me!? You must never
doubt me again!
Mank laughs

MANK
It's good, huh?

WELLES
Good?! Good?! Words fail you at last! It's terrific! Now I'll have to do some shaping,
of course, and some of the scenes aren't exactly ...exactly . . .

MANK
What?

WELLES
Short enough. But this is a grand start And I think we need to change the name.

MANK
The title?

WELLES
No, AMERICAN is a blessed title directly sent from
God's soul to your mind. We shall never change that!
I mean the name of the publisher. Charles Foster
Craig doesn't have the knives-out poetry I need. I was thinking about "Kane" -- you like
that?

MANK
Cain -- like the Bible guy?

WELLES
K-A-N-E. One strong syllable. Kane I

MANK
(weakly)Craig is one syllable

WELLES
But it's not a great syllable

Houseman returns with a tray of drinks. Welles hands glasses all around as:

MANK
I --um-- I don't know if I should. I ain't been drinking since I started on this--

WELLES
(toasting)
To my invaluable comrade Drink up!
Mank is stunned Welles smiles and drinks.

INT CAR. DESERT ROADS DAY
Welles sits in the back of his limo as his chauffeur speeds him back to
Los Angeles.
He goes through the script with a fervent intensity. He crosses out huge sections and
tosses away entire pages. The' floor around his feet is littered with discarded pages.
Mank sits drinking heavily as the sun sets in the distance Houseman is busy packing in
the house behind him.
Houseman notices Mank and goes to him They stare at the crimson of the setting sun
for a moment

MANK
I'm out, aren't I?

HOUSEMAN
Welcome to the world of Orson Welles.
We focus on Mank's glowering face. But the background is somehow different. We are
at...

INT MANK'S CAR NIGHT
Late at night. Mank is sitting in his car, drinking from his flask and listening to period
jazz music from the car radio. He is parked outside
Welles' house, waiting and seething and very drunk.
He sees Welles pulling into his driveway and climbing out of his car.
Mank takes a final swig and then bolts after him, carrying a script. .

.

EXT WELLES ' HOUSE FOLLOWING
Mank roars unsteadily up to Welles:

MANK
YOU FUCK! YOU SELFISH FUCK!
Mank flings the script in Welles' face. Welles recoils

WELLES
Jesus Christ --

MANK
**YOU CAN'T DO THIS TOME -- THIS WAS OUR STORY,
REMEMBER? -- YOU AND ME AND GODDAMN EVERYONE ELSE -
- REMEMBER THAT?!**
Mank snatches up the script and thrusts it in Welles' face

MANK
Pal from the studio sent this -- you see that?!
What does it say?! WHAT DOES IT SAY ORSON?!
Welles bats the script away:

WELLES
Get away from me--
Mank pushes the title page of the script toward Welles as

MANX
It says AMERICAN by Orson Welles. YOU TOOK MY NAME

OFF THE FUCKING SCRIPT!
WELLES
It's obviously a mistake, Manki Some steno girl made a mistake, alright?!

MANK
You can't do this to me--!
Welles spins on him:

WELLES
(savagely)
I fucking well can! I own your script and I can do anything I goddamn want. And don't
forget for one minute that I took your 350 pages of drunken rambling and I made a
movie out of them -- and now
I've got to shoot the bastard. So thank you very much, I have all I need. And you can
stop calling me.
He goes into his house and slams the door.
Mank leans against the door in stunned exhaustion. Then he slides down the door and
sits leaning against it.

MANK
(quietly)
I hope you choke on it. I hope it kills you.
Inside the darkened House, Welles is leaning against the front door.
Silent.

INT ,, SAM SIMEON. ASSEMBLY RQOM NIGHT
The Assembly room is Hearst's private sanctum high in a tower at San
Simeon.

Marion is valiantly trying to piece together a huge jigsaw puzzle.
Hearst enters and goes to her. He puts his hand gently on her shoulder.

MARION
This is supposed ta be Siam or some such. Some kinda lousy B-B-Balinese temple. This
look like a temple to you? I can't see it myself--

HEARST
(quietly)
Darling, I talked to Millicent.
Marion stops working at the puzzle. She does not look up. Beat

HEARST
She said no
A pause. Then:
Marion slowly reaches out for the puzzle and delicately place a piece in the proper
position.

MARION
There. That's right.

HEARST
She's a Catholic. She says it would put her soul in peril. Divorce is a very serious sin,
apparently.

MARION
(not looking up)
Nuts. She only cares about the money. She thinks
I'll make you cut her out of the w-w-w-w...
(she clenches her fists) will.
A long, difficult pause

HEARST
I'm so sorry.
Marion slowly stands and walks to a liquor cabinet and pours a stiff drink.
Hearst watches sadly, but doesn't say a word

INT SCHAEFER'S OFFICE. RKO LOT DAY
Welles paces before Schaefer's massive desk with typical combustible energy. Behind
the desk, huge picture windows show the bustling activities of the RKO lot.

WELLES
It's an awful title, of course, but I can't think of anything better. Someone came up with
A SEA OF
UPTURNED FACES -- which has a nice, grand ring to it

-- and I thought of JOHN CITIZEN, USA but that strikes me as a bit Warner Brothers. Or, God forbid,
Capraesque. I suppose AMERICAN will do for now but--

SCHAEFER
CITIZEN KANE
WELLES
Pardon?

SCHAEFER
CITIZEN KANE There's your title.
Welles muses

WELLES
A "Z" and a "K" in the title. That would draw the eye. For the poster. I like that THE PRISONER OF
ZENDA had a "Z" and a "P" and that worked--

SCHAEFER
Now look, Orson, let's not get ahead of ourselves.
The budget projections on this--

WELLES
(theatrically)
I know, I know! But what more can you expect of me?! I have pared this story down to the marrow to save money but to cut more would be to--!

SCHAEFER
Listen, get off your horse with me. You know I've stuck by you since the beginning of time it seems like, while the stockholders in New York were ready to cut and run and everyone else in Hollywood was set to toss me in a rubber room. But your contract stipulates a max budget of 500 thousand. This one's gonna come in at 750 thousand. What do we do about that?
A beat

SCHAEFER
Now don't have a fit -- but I want you to think again about doing WAR OF THE WORLDS-

WELLES
Jesus

SCHAEFER
Do WAR OF THE WORLDS as a feature and everyone's happy. You make some money and New York's happy and you have a track record and then we'll move on to

KANE.
WELLES
Please don't ask me to do this.

SCHAEFER
It's the safe bet, Orson. There's nothing wrong with that.
A long pause as Welles leans against a wall, his head down He does not look at Schaefer as:

WELLES
(simply)
George, I want you to let me make this movie because I need to make it. And I don't really know why. Afterwards there' II be all the time in the world to make money and sell popcorn. And I'll do that for you. For RKO and New York. But for now ... please let me tell this story.
A beat. Welles finally looks up at Schaefer

WELLES
It's your decision, George. If you look into my eyes right now and say, go make WAR OF THE WORLDS, I will. I'll make it. And, yes, it'll make you money.
And I honestly can't think of a reason in the world why you should let me do KANE other than that you should.
A long pause as Schaefer studies Welles. Then

SCHAEFER
If it'll get you the hell out of my office, go ahead and make the picture.
Welles drops his head, too moved to speak.
Then he nods to Schaefer and begins to leave.

SCHAEFER
Say thank you, Orson.
Welles glances at him.

SCHAEFER
For the title

WELLES
(smiles)
Ah, it's a grand title.
He sweeps out. Schaefer smiles and shakes his head.

SCHAEFER
Like it would kill him to say thank you

EXT SOUND STAGE. RKO LOT DAWN

The sun is just rising on the RKO lot. We note a sign on the wall by the sound stage door:

CITIZEN KANE. RKO PRODUCTION #281. DIRECTOR: ORSON WELLES
ABSOLUTELY NO
ADMITTANCE.
INT RKO SOUND STAGE FOLLOWING
Absolute silence.

Welles stands in the mammoth sound stage and looks around, it is as if he has entered a great cathedral. A few lights illuminate portions of the stage and giant lighting rigs and scaffolding soar to the unseen ceiling miles away.

The Xanadu Great Hall set awaits.

Welles slowly walks to the set and stands, surveying his domain, savoring the moment. Title: JULY 30, 1940

He clears his throat and speaks, rehearsing his first day speech to the cast and crew. His voice echoes.

WELLES
Today we - -
He stops, surprised by the echo.

WELLES
Today we are going to break every rule in motion picture history...
No . . We are going to shatter every rule in
Today we are going to shatter the hallowed busts of Griffith and
DeMille and Ford. We are going to show the world a new way of seeing.
Together we will blaze a trail...
As Welles continues to rehearse we slowly ascend the scaffolding and lighting rigs...

WELLES' VOICE
Together we will throw away all the maps and we will become -joyously lost in the wilderness. And the future cartographers of Hollywood will forever chart our course. Following our lead...

We continue to ascend and finally discover two electricians on the upper catwalk, staring down in amusement, much like the two stagehands at the opera in KANE.

WELLES' VOICE
And do you know why we're going to do this?
Again to Welles on the stage floor: A beat. Welles slowly smiles.

WELLES
We're going to do this because it's going to be fun.
Above, one of the electrician's throws the switch on a huge spotlight.

Welles is captured in the vibrant white light and Benny Goodman's immortal "SING, SING, SING" immediately explodes and we are into:

THE MAKING OF CITIZEN KANE
A camera crane sweeps dramatically to the ceiling of the sound stage and brilliant white lights flash on.
A film clapper snaps: CITIZEN KANE. RKO PRODUCTION 281 DIRECTOR:

**ORSON
WELLES.**
And we see Welles racing heroically into making his first movie:
In varying KANE makeups he tears through scenes and actors: laughing with AGNES MOOREHEAD on the cabin set; charming RUTH WARRICK on the breakfast table set; berating DOROTHY COMMINGORE on the Great Hall set...
He speeds back and forth and back and forth from the set to the camera in the Campaign Headquarters set, never happy with the shot. . .
Gregg Toland watches, bemused, as Welles shifts tiny prop pieces on the set. . .
Welles bullies and screams and pleads and seduces. Like an obsessed artistic tornado he is seemingly everywhere at once. We see him rejecting matte paintings and in makeup and rewriting the script and trying on costumes and selecting props and leaping into odd positions looking for the perfect camera angle.
It is very important in this sequence that we see the pressure building
... building ... building ... on Welles.
"SING, SING, SING" continues On the Xanadu stairway set Welles behind the camera, filming actor Paul Stewart

PAUL STEWART
"Rosebud? I'll tell you about Rosebud.

WELLES
Again.
A film clapper: take 58

PAUL STEWART
"Rosebud? I'll tell you about Rosebud.

WELLES
Again.
A film clapper: take 59

PAUL STEWART
"Rosebud? I'll tell you about Rosebud.

WELLES
Again
"SING. SING, SING" continues... in a corner of the sound stage:
Welles, in full Kane makeup, studies a miniature model of the Kane
Campaign Headquarters set through a tiny periscope with cinematographer
Gregg Toland.

WELLES
It needs a ceiling, Gregg. Real rooms have real ceilings.

GREGG TOLAND
You want a ceiling on this one too?

WELLES
You bet.

GREGG TOLAND
Gonna be tough

WELLES
(smiles)
No, it's gonna be impossible. That's why we're doing it.
SING, SING, SING" continues Back on the Xanadu stairway set: Poor Paul
Stewart, now at his wit's ends, continues:

PAUL STEWART
"Rosebud? I'll tell you about Rosebud."

WELLES
Again
The film clapper: take 112.

PAUL STEWART
"Rosebud? I'll tell you about Rosebud

WELLES
Again
Paul Stewart screams and collapses. "SING, SING, SING" continues... On the Atlantic
City nightclub set:
Welles watches as the camera crane attempts the dizzying and difficult maneuver from
the skylight at the top of the set down to Dorothy Commingore as Susan Alexander
below. The camera crane goes out of control and crashes through some light fixtures
and swings crazily down toward Dorothy Commingore. She yelps and leaps away as
the camera barrels through the table and smashes to the floor.
Welles stands next to Toland. A beat.

WELLES
Well, that didn't really work
"SING, SING, SING" continues. Back on the, Xanadu stairway set
Paul Stewart, dazed and shattered, is listening intently. Welles stands with his arms
around Stewart, embracing him, whispering into his ear.

WELLES
It is the most important line of the picture. You will weave the magic of "Rosebud" in a single word -
- you will say the word in such a way as to impart to us the mystery of it. It is a divine and sinister mystery worthy only of your talent. In this one word the movie soars or falls. Once more, I beg you.
Stewart nods. The film clapper: take 178.
The cameraman leans into the viewfinder. We see his black- and-white view of the shot through the lens then:
In a cramped editing room we see Welles watching the scene on an old editing moviola. On the moviola we see Paul Stewart taking a deep breath and then, magnificently:

PAUL STEWART
(On moviola)
"Rosebud? I'll tell you about Rosebud."

WELLES' VOICE
(On moviola)
Print. ;'
On the moviola we see Stewart laugh hysterically and dance away.
In the editing room, Welles shakes his head

WELLES
Actors.
"SING, SING, SING" continues. On the Campaign Headquarters set:
Welles and Toland lie on the floor of the Campaign Headquarters set and gaze up through viewfinders. They squirm about on the floor and laugh to one another about their newest outlandish idea.
Then Toland notices something in the catwalks high above the set. A redheaded ELECTRICIAN.
TOLAND Orson, you see that electrician up there? The redhead.
He was on GRAPES OF WRATH. He's a free- lance studio spy. Probably reports right back to the RKO boys in New York.
Welles slowly stands and THUNDERS:

WELLES
STOP EVERYBODY STOP!
All the flurried activity on the sound stage immediately stops.
Every eye turns, terrified, to Welles. Welles glares up at the redheaded electrician

WELLES
YOU COME DOWN HERE!
The electrician slowly climbs down from the rafters. Welles rivets him every step of the way.
The electrician stops before Welles.

ELECTRICIAN

Mr. Welles...?

A tense beat and then Welles fiercely and purposefully spits in the electrician's face. The electrician recoils, stunned.

WELLES
GET OUT

Welles returns to Toland as the electrician slinks off "SING, SING, SING" continues as:

We see the magnificent film emerging. Welles watching scenes in a screening room, his feet up, exhausted, almost asleep, a cigar dangling from his lips...

We see rushes of Welles going through scenes with Dorothy Commingore as Susan Alexander. He is relentless with her off camera, driving her to the harridan outbursts he wants just before he steps into the shot...

We see the crew observing, with great amusement, Welles' stumbling attempts to learn the "Charlie Kane" dance...

We see Toland shifting lights to achieve deep-focus cross-fades. Welles rages as the difficult process eats up time...

We see Welles growing increasingly manic. The long hours and the pressure are clearly taking a toll..

We return to the screening room. Welles is now fully asleep. His cigar falls from his mouth and begins smoldering on his suit.

"SING, SING, SING" fades at... On a Xanadu set:

Filming a scene. Welles, in old-Kane makeup, is sitting with Dorothy Commingore as Susan Alexander. He is curiously distracted. She is pouring tea in the scene:

DOROTHY COMMINGORE

"Charlie, you sure got the funniest ways of looking at things . "

Welles does not respond. He breaks character

WELLES

No -- no -- I'll pour the tea. Sorry. I should pour the tea. Let's try that again.

Toland stands behind the camera and watches Welles. There is obviously something wrong.

WELLES

Okay, here we go... Set. Action

Welles pops into character and pours the tea in the scene as:

DOROTHY COMMINGORE

"Charlie, you sure got the funniest ways of looking at things . "

Welles stops, breaks character again:

WELLES

No -- that's not right

He clears his throat and glances at the enormous crew, all staring back at him expectantly.

WELLES
Urn...ah ...yes -- you should definitely pour the tea. Okay, again. Sorry.... Set. Action.
They start the scene again. She pours the tea

DOROTHY COMMINGORE
"Charlie, you sure got the funniest ways of looking at things . "
A pause as she waits for his reply in the scene He sits, frozen.

TOLAND
Orson, you wanna take five?

WELLES
Five...? Yes. No. We're done today
He slowly walks off the set as he nervously pulls at his tie, tearing it off.
Toland watches him go.

INT BROWN DERBY DAY
Louella is at her usual corner booth, on the phone to one of her many spies. She is devouring a Cobb salad as she hears:'

PHONE VOICE
I don't know if this means anything but I just talked to a guy in the RKO art department
They've got all these books and crap all over the place.
Pictures of San Simeon.
Louella instantly stops eating

PHONE VOICE
For the Welles picture.

LOUELLA
Pictures of the castle?

PHONE VOICE
Yeah

LOUELLA
Thanks, doll. Get me more.
She hangs up, intrigued.

INT WELLES' HOUSE
Welles is standing, absolutely lost, in the middle of his living room.
He is still in his old-Kane makeup which is just beginning to peel off his face.
We hear a low, insistent drum beat, a Gene Krupa riff.

We hear the sound of an ice pick chipping into a block of ice. Welles glances around. We are no longer in Welles' living room but at. . .

INT MANK'S HOUSE. SANTA MONICA DAY
A turntable spins in a corner, playing a Gene Krupa record. Ashtrays overflow with cigar butts and messy piles of pages are littered around a typewriter.
Mank's beach house is tiny and on the edge of squalid
Welles, still in his peeling old-Kane makeup, is standing in the middle of the living room and Mank is in the small kitchenette, chipping ice for drinks.
A long pause

WELLES
And I'm looking at them -- and they're all looking at me and I don't know who should pour the tea. '

MANK
Uh huh.

WELLES
I just can't . . see it anymore
Mank returns to the living room and thrusts a drink in Welles hand.

WELLES
I want you back

MANK
Fuck you. (He sits.) You wanted me out. I'm out.

WELLES
I'm sorry.

MANK
I don't care.
Welles hands Mank a folded script from his jacket. Mank looks at it as:

WELLES
This is the shooting script we've been using every day.
Sure enough, the title page of the script reads: CITIZEN KANE by Herman J. Mankiewicz and Orson Welles.

WELLES
It's just like we always said it would be
Mank hands it back

MANK
Too late, kid.

Welles sits.

WELLES
Did I ever tell you about my father?

MANK
I don't give a shit about-

WELLES
He was a drunk. And he was my father and I was ashamed of him.
A beat. Welles proceeds quietly and with difficulty.

WELLES
He showed me the world, he took me with him everywhere -- Europe, China -- and he was so proud of me. But he would drink and he would get
...embarrassing. And I began to resent him Because I was so ... sparkling, you see.
So I cut him dead. I turned my back and I walked away because I didn't need him. He was getting in the way of my "genius." And he would write me letters, and I never answered them, and he would call me, and I never took his calls, and he showed up at school and I wouldn't see him.
Tears are beginning to inch down Welles' face

WELLES
When I finally saw him again, he was in a coffin. I was fifteen. And all of a sudden he wasn't that embarrassing drunk anymore ... he was the man who showed me the world.
Welles looks up at Mank, tears now streaming down his face.

WELLES
Just like you, Mank.
A long beat. Mank, despite himself, is moved.
To cover his emotion Mank rises and goes into the kitchen to freshen his drink. We remain tight on Welles as we hear Mank's voice:

MANK'S VOICE
So you've lost it? Don't know who should pour the tea.

WELLES
Yeah
A beat

MANK'S VOICE
Orson ... just cut the goddamn tea

WELLES
Okay
A beat. Welles reaches for a cigar, tears still wet on his face.

MANK'S VOICE
I been thinking about the beach scene. You done that yet?

WELLES
No

MANK'S VOICE
Good -- cause I was thinking that we're starting the scene too late...
Welles quickly bites off the end of his cigar -- his expression one of
"Gotcha!" -- even as. his cheeks are still wet with tears.

MANK'S VOICE (CONT.)
Cause if we don't show Susan watching Kane more then we're not building the right
tension into the scene. See, she's gotta know that...
Welles slowly smiles as the record of Gene Krupa's percussion segues into the
unmistakable rhythms of "SING, SING, SING" and eclipses Mank's voice...
And we see Welles everywhere, more energized than ever: perilous on a high crane;
stuck in a cramped corner behind the camera; doing magic tricks for the cast; sleeping
as makeup is applied to his face...
Mank is always at Welles' side: supporting; challenging; amusing; inspiring. . .
We see Welles strutting, raging, boasting, dancing. And again towering.
"SING, SING, SING" finally ends at..
Through the black-and-white viewfinder we see Welles, in full costume and makeup,
carefully walking across the massive Kane Campaign
Headquarters set toward us. We see the low angle black-and-white camera's
perspective.

TOLAND'S VOICE
Closer ... closer ... closer -- stop. We just lost your head.

WELLES
Can you see my shoes?

TOLAND'S VOICE
Yeah, but we lose your head.

WELLES
Goddamn it Joe -- stand here
JOSEPH COTTON, also in full costume and makeup, steps into the shot and takes
Welles' position as Welles scurries out of the frame. . ..

INT SOUND STAGE. RKO NIGHT. FOLLOWING
Welles marches across the set and squirms into position at the camera, which is right
on the floor, and peers up through the viewfinder.
Toland lies next to him. Mank stands to one side and- watches.

WELLES
It's just not low enough. This is the scene. We have to look up at these two man as pillars soaring to the sky. As towering virtues in combat--

TOLAND
Spare me the aria, I know what you want--

WELLES
I need my shoes in total focus right here and also
Joe back there--!

TOLAND
I know what you want but it can't be done!

WELLES
Take apart the fucking camera rig -- we could get a few more inches down and then tilt up--

TOLAND
Orson -- we can't get the fucking camera any fucking lower so find another fucking shot!
Welles thinks for a moment and then bolts up. Toland watches, mystified, as Welles races to a sound stage fire station and grabs a fire axe. Welles storms back to the set and raises the axe high. Toland quickly rolls away. And Welles slams the axe into the wooden floor of the set. He continues to hack at the floor.

WELLES
Come on, Gregg! We'll tear out this floor!
Welles and Toland and various grips hack at the floor
Mank watches, bemused, and checks his watch
Welles and Toland finally tear away the remnants of the wooden floor.
They stare down, defeated. Under the wood is solid concrete.
Welles and Toland stand and stare at the concrete

TOLAND
It's midnight, why don't we pick it up tomorrow?
Welles does not answer. He continues to eye the concrete Then:

WELLES
Get me a jackhammer.
We see a grip pounding away at the concrete with a jackhammer as
Welles, always in motion, sweeps past Mank and Joseph Cotton.

MANK
(wryly, to Cotton)

There but for the grace of God, goes God.
Welles slams to a halt in front of the unit physician and thrusts out an arm. The physician injects him with a dose of B-12.
Welles can barely wait for the injection before he speeds off.
Welles supervises as Toland lowers the camera into the freshly dug hole in the middle of the sound stage. Mank checks his watch, 3:30 AM.
Welles leaps into the trench to check the camera setup.
Again we see the view through the black-and-white viewfinder. Joseph
Cotton stands at a distance, at the far wall of the set.

WELLES' VOICE
Okay, Joe ...come closer ...closer
We see Cotton approaching. He finally stops inches away from the camera. His shoes and the far wall of the set are both in total focus.
It is a breathtaking, vertiginous shot.
Then we see Welles and Joseph Cotton rehearsing and rehearsing and filming and filming the scene. Endlessly
Finally we seem to be seeing the scene from the movie

WELLES
"Well, if you got drunk to talk to me about Miss
Alexander, don't bother. I'm not interested. I've set back the sacred cause of reform, is that it? All right, if that's the way they want it, the people have made their choice. It's obvious the people prefer Jim Gettys to me."

JOSEPH COTTON
"You talk about the people as if you owned them. As though they belonged to you. As long as I can remember, you've talked about--" (he breaks character)
Orson, I am so goddamn tired--
We continue to watch the scene through the viewfinder:

WELLES
(to the camera operator)
Keep filming.

JOSEPH COTTON
I can't remember the lines!

WELLES
Then make them up! You're drunk and you're angry.
He shoves Joseph Cotton brutally

WELLES
This is the chance you've been waiting for, boy.
Tell that son of a bitch just what you think of him!

JOSEPH COTTON
We're not all hopped up on benzedrine, Orson I Some of us humans need sleep!
Welles shoves him again.

WELLES
You're not going to get another chance, boy! Look right at the monster and you tell him-
-

JOSEPH COTTON
(deeply)
"You don't care about anything except you. You just want to persuade people that you

JOSEPH COTTON (CONT.) love them so much that they ought to love you back.
Only you want love on your own terms. "

WELLES
"A toast then, Jedediah, to love on my own terms.
Those are the only terms anybody ever knows, his own."
Welles/Kane drinks. A long pause.

WELLES
Cut. Print
We jump out of the black-and-white viewfinder and into the scene as
Welles turns to an assistant.

WELLES
How 'bout a real drink?

TOLAND
We done?

WELLES
Yeah.
The crew members exhale and practically collapse
Welles stands and looks around in satisfaction. He takes in the empty corners of the
sound stage, the sets, the cameras Savoring the moment.

WELLES
(quietly)
It's finished.
He walks to the massive doors of the sound stage and pulls them open.
Sunlight floods in.
Outside it is a blazing morning and the dazzling sunlight silhouettes
Welles.

Welles squints and steps into the glorious sunlight. Mank and Toland follow. They stand and watch as RKO extras and crews bustle about on their way to work. The assistant brings a tray of martinis.
They each take a glass. The RKO workers stare at them oddly as they pass.
Welles toasts them.

WELLES
Good morning, good morning. . .
He grabs a passing extra and dances with her as Mank and Toland laugh.

EXT HEDDA'S MANSION. PATIO MORNING
Hedda Hopper reclines on her patio. An extremely ugly pug dog sits in her lap. She has green goo all over her face and a cigarette dangling from her lips.
Title: THREE MONTHS LATER. JANUARY 3, 1941
She is going through the trades. She stops at a particular item. She studies it and then reaches for the phone and dials.

HEDDA
(on phone)
Orson, Hedda here! You naughty boy! You told me that I would be positively the first human soul to see your masterpiece and here I read in the Reporter that there's a screening tonight for the magazines
... yes, advance deadlines, I understand ...(she smiles) ...oh, rough cut, uh-huh ... Been there,
Orson, know the drill. See ya tonight!
She hangs up. Her hideous dog leaps on her and starts licking her face goo.

HEDDA
Get offa me, ya little prick

INT OUTSIDE AN RKO SCREENING ROOM NIGHT
Welles paces nervously outside the doors to the screening room.
Schaefer stands leaning against a wall.
From inside we can hear some of the final dialogue from CITIZEN KANE.

WELLES
This is an abomination There's no music and--

SCHAEFER
They've all seen a rough cut

WELLES
The magazines are one thing -- but Hedda! Why did we have to let her come?!

SCHAEFER
When Hedda says "I'm coming" you mix a lot of martinis and you pray.

Silence from inside the screening room. The movie is over. An agonizing silent pause
Then the doors swing open and the guests stream out. Totally neutral expressions.
The bejeweled Valkyrie, Hedda herself, finally emerges. She stops before Welles.
A beat.
She reaches up and pinches his cheek, a bit too hard. And then she slaps his cheek, a bit
too hard.
And then she goes

WELLES
What the hell did that mean?!

EXT HEDDA' S MANSION. PATIO MORNING
Hedda paces and smokes as she waits on the phone. Finally, she is connected:

HEDDA
(brightly)
Why hello, Mr. Hearst! I'm so delighted you could take my call. I just wanted to let you
know -- I saw this Orson Welles picture last night. First screening ever, don't cha know,
and, Mr. Hearst, I don't understand something ...(she smiles wickedly) ... I just don't
understand why Louella hasn't told you it ' s all about you...Yes, oh yes ...My pleasure,
sir.
She hangs up

HEDDA
Take that, you old cow

INT SCHAEFER'S OFFICE DAY
Schaefer sits at his desk, going through some budget sheets. His intercom buzzes, he
presses a button:
SECRETARY'S VOICE Mr. Schaefer, Miss Parsons is here

SCHAEFER
(into intercom)
Here? As in right outside the door?

SECRETARY'S VOICE
Yes, sir

SCHAEFER
(chipper, into intercom)
Well, send her in!
He releases his intercom button

SCHAEFER
Shit

He bolts up and races to the liquor cabinet as Louella sweeps in like the Lusitania in fur.

LOUELLA
Schaefer, I gotta see this Welles picture

SCHAEFER
Louella, hello, I was just fixing a drink, would you like--?

LOUELLA
(eyeing gossip)
You drink at 10 am, do you?

SCHAEFER
No -- no -- I mean--

LOUELLA
I wanna see the picture today

SCHAEFER
That might be a tad difficult because Orson is scoring the picture now and he's very particular about the music--

LOUELLA
Cut the malarkey, buddy. The boss himself wants me to see the picture today.

SCHAEFER
He personally asked you to?

LOUELLA
That's right
Beat

SCHAEFER
Hearst?

LOUELLA
Uh-huh
Beat

LOUELLA
I'll be back at noon. Set it up in screening room four.
She sweeps out

SCHAEFER
Oh god

INT RKO SCREENING ROOM DAY
Louella watches CITIZEN KANE
We watch her enormous face, grim and glowering, bathed in flickering blue light as we hear a bit of the dialogue:

" KANE "
"You'll continue with your singing, Susan. I don't propose to have myself made ridiculous. "

"SUSAN ALEXANDER"
"You don't propose to have yourself made ridiculous
I What about me?! I'm the one that's got to do the singing! I'm the one who gets the razzberries!"
With that, Louella bolts up and stomps out of the screening^ room... '

INT OUTSIDE THE SCREENING ROOM FOLLOWING
Welles and Schaefer are again nervously waiting in the hallway.
Louella slams out the door and almost crashes into Welles A beat as she glares at him.
If looks could kill She storms off
Welles and Schaefer are too stunned even to speak as we hear:

LOUELLA'S VOICE
It is ...assassination.

INT SAN SIMEON. ASSEMBLY ROOM DAY
Hearst sits with one of his dachshunds on his lap Louella sits across from him.
Hearst does not move a muscle in the entire scene.

LOUELLA (CONT.)
It's all you. It has the political campaigns and the mining fortune and the war with Pulitzer and the castle. And ... Marion.

HEARST
How so?

LOUELLA
The jigsaw puzzles and the, urn, career -- the man spending a fortune to make her a star -- only it's opera and not movies. And...

HEARST
Yes?

LOUELLA
(quietly)
The drinking.

A beat

HEARST
(very controlled)
So my life is a subject for mockery. All of it.
Every detail. Every personal detail.
Louella nods.
A beat.

HEARST
Thank you for your time

LOUELLA
Thank you, sir. She begins to leave
A beat
A pause

HEARST
Miss Parsons, I have one additional question for you.

LOUELLA
Sir?
(stops)

HEARST
Why did we not know about this sooner?

LOUELLA
Sir?

HEARST
I pay you a good deal of money to be my eyes and ears in Hollywood, do I not? If you
cannot provide this simple service you are of no use to me.

LOUELLA
Sir, I-

HEARST
(lethally)
Please be quiet.
A young man has made a motion picture detailing my life. This motion picture was
made at a not insignificant studio. And you knew nothing about it.

LOUELLA
He lied to me

LOUELLA
He looked into my face and told me it wasn't about you.

HEARST
And how do you feel when you are lied to?
A beat.

LOUELLA
I want blood

HEARST
Good. Retain that feeling. Let it nourish you from this day forth. It shall nourish us both
She nods and leaves the room We linger on Hearst, his expression dark and dangerous.

INT SCHAEFER'S OFFICE EVENING
Welles reclines on a sofa, smoking a cigar, orating, while Schaefer sits at his desk absently flipping through the evening edition of the

LA EXAMINER.
WELLES
Give me one dinner with her and I'll sort it out.
Woman of a certain age are woefully susceptible to a younger man's charm. I'll make myself so monumentally attractive that
He is distracted by Schaefer flipping through the newspaper anxiously.
Schaefer tears back and forth in the paper and then swivels around in his chair to grab another newspaper. He flips through it. And then stops.

SCHAEFER
(sickened)
Oh Christ...
Welles leaps up and goes to Schaefer's desk.
Schaefer has placed the two newspapers side by side on his desk.
He points to one

SCHAEFER
This is the morning edition of the EXAMINER.
He points to the other

SCHAEFER
And this is the evening edition. Notice anything?

WELLES
The ad..
Indeed, the morning edition contains a large ad for the RKO movie KITTY FOYLE. In the evening edition the ad has been replaced by innocuous copy.

SCHAEFER
They dumped our ad.
He flips through the evening edition and then looks up at Welles.

SCHAEFER
(quietly)
They dumped all our ads.

INT MAYER'S OFFICE DAY
Louis B. Mayer sits at his massive desk, taking notes Hearst sweeps in.
Mayer is surprised.

HEARST
Louis

MAYER
Randolph!

HEARST
Hope you don't mind my popping in--

MAYER
No -- no -- sit down, please

HEARST
(sitting)
What a wretched place this is. I can't come to town without feeling filthy. You really
must buy that parcel of land by the castle and come north.
I only wish I could. You know, business

HEARST
Quite. And this is why I came to visit. Have you heard about this CITIZEN KANE
picture?

MAYER
Over at RKO?
A beat.

HEARST
Mm. Not a very good picture I am told.

MAYER
(confused)
Uh-hub.

HEARST

Apparently it details the exploits of a publisher like myself. Entirely too much like myself. Do you follow so far?

MAYER
Yeah
A beat.

HEARST
I can't see how the release of that picture will do anyone any good, really.

HEARST
Say, while I'm in town why don't we play 18 holes at Bel Air? Or maybe just nine. Do you have time for a round today?
He gazes at Mayer. Mayer looks at him, disquieted
A pause.
A beat

HEARST
And maybe we could get Mr. Warner and Mr. Goldwyn and Mr. Cohn and Mr. Selznick to play as well.

MAYER
(quietly)
You know that can't happen.

HEARST
Oh, why is that?

HEARST
Why is that, Louis?

MAYER
Bel Air is restricted.

HEARST
Oh, that's right. How silly of me to have forgotten. I sometimes forget that you're all Jews.
Lots of people forget that. If they ever knew it.
A tense pause

HEARST
See what you can do about this CITIZEN KANE picture, won't you?

MAYER
(quietly)
Yeah

Hearst stands.

HEARST
And you'll come out to the castle soon, I hope
Marion and I would love to see more of you.
He smiles and goes. Mayer sits, shaken

INT BROWN DERBY NIGHT
Schaefer sits with Louella in her corner booth

LOUELLA
That's right, fella, no Hearst paper will run an
RKO ad until you agree that CITIZEN KANE will never see the light of day.

SCHAEFER
Louella, please, be reasonable, I understand you have problems with Orson's picture but
maybe we can work something out--

LOUELLA
Nix, sweetie. You shelve it

SCHAEFER
Oh for God's sake, Louella-

LOUELLA
And Mr. Hearst has authorized me to tell you that you're looking at the most beautiful
lawsuit in history if you release this picture. He'll bleed your little studio dry and you
can all go on back to
New York and do Shakespeare with the Boy Wonder.

SCHAEFER
Can I talk to Hearst?

LOUELLA
You are talking to him.

INT SAN SIMEON. ASSEMBLY ROOM DAY
Hearst stands with his arms behind his back, very Kane-like, and surveys a collection
of about 30 newspapers spread around the floor at his feet. His newspapers.
Marion sits in a corner, doing needlepoint. Hearst picks up one of his papers

HEARST
The Journal was pretty harsh to Roosevelt today.

MARION
You oughta lay off him -- he is the p-p-president, after all.

HEARST
He is a Bolshevik. He will have us at war by the end of the year. I think I'm going to
run that wheelchair picture.

MARION
Don't
She holds up her needlepoint

MARION
Whaddaya think?
It is a sampler reading: BLESS THIS CASTLE He laughs
JOE WILLICOMBE, Hearst's private secretary, enters quietly. Willicombe is a serious
and sensitive man in his 60's. He is unquestioningly loyal to the old man.

WILLICOMBE
Sir, we got the call.
A moment. Hearst looks at him. Willicombe shakes his head sadly.

HEARST
Thank you, Joseph.
Willicombe glides out
A long pause as Hearst moves to a window and stares down at his domain.
Marion watches him.

MARION
How bad is it?

HEARST
Nothing for you to worry about, darling

MARION
Pops
A beat

HEARST
The S.E.C. has turned down my request for relief on the debts.

MARION
How much?

HEARST
It's not really--

MARION
How much?

A -beat

HEARST
125 million.
She is absolutely stunned. A pause

MARION
(softly)
We're 125 million dollars in debt?

HEARST
Yes.
A pause
Hearst continues to gaze out the window. Marion goes to him and holds him tenderly. ;
They look down at the massive San Simeon estate spreading out like
Wonderland below them.

INT
MARION
How does one get 125 million dollars in debt?

HEARST
One ...buys things.

INT RECORDING STAGE NIGHT
KANE composer BERNARD HERMANN stands before an orchestra, going over some
of the music for KANE. He tries various measures and makes adjustments. A movie
screen is ready to run sections of the film.
Welles sits at the back of the room, talking quietly to Gregg Toland.
Welles is bewitching, spinning a web:

WELLES
We open on Monument Valley. Those towering stalagmites reaching up like pleading
fingers to
God. A single figure treads the arid plains. The crimson sun is behind him so his shadow
stretches toward us. He is a simple man wearing a simple robe.
A profoundly quiet and sad man. Who is he?
Bernard Hermann turns back to Welles and Toland

BERNARD HERMANN
Orson, please..

WELLES
(whispering, to Toland)
Who is he, Gregg?

TOLAND
(realizing)
Oh, no--

WELLES
Yes!

TOLAND
He's Christ?

WELLES
I'm Christ

TOLAND
You want to do the life of Jesus?

WELLES
Yes! Vibrant and modern and stark like a Picasso sketch drawn to flashes of lightning I
We shoot the whole thing in the gallant American West--
Mank joins them, carrying a newspaper.

MANK
Hey, kid. Gregg.

WELLES
Mank, sit down. You missed the opening of the new picture but I'll go back--

MANK
No, you gotta hear this-

BERNARD HERMANN
(snapping back at them)
I'm trying to work here!

WELLES
Sorry, you keep at it, old boy.
He leads Toland and Mank out of the stage and into the sound proof recording booth...

INT. SOUND BOOTH
A few sound engineers and mixers work over recording panels and watch
Hermann and the orchestra as Welles, Toland and Mank enter.

MANK
You read Louella?
Welles shudders

WELLES
No, but I can imagine. What am I today? A "puny upstart" or a "spoiled dilettante" --
no, she wouldn't know how to spell that

MANK
(reads)
"And how is the country to feel when this industry continues to employ bedraggled
foreigners and swarthy refugees instead of real Americans? Doesn't
Hollywood know there's a Depression on? Don't real
Americans deserve work?"

WELLES
(laughs)
Well, at least she's off KANE today

MANK
No she's not. Don't you get it, ya lunk? She's using code language to the studio bosses.
"Bedraggled foreigners and swarthy refugees" -- who the hell do you think she's talking
about?

WELLES
(playfully)
Hedy Lamarr?

MANK
Jews. She's talking about Jews. beat
Welles' smile fades.

MANK
Who owns this town? Who runs every goddamn studio?
The tribe, baby. These fuckers hear the word "Jew" and they start sweating. Like Ester
Williams' pool they start sweating.

WELLES
(growing tense)
So they're Jews. . .

MANK
This is just the first shot. Maestro. Sooner or later she's gonna use the word. And all
those boys know that there is only one thing this country hates more than the coloreds
and that's the Jews.

WELLES
Christ.

MANK

Me, I'm proud to be a Jew, I got no problem. You don't like it, fuck you. But with these guys it's like a dirty word. All they wanna be is good red- white-and-blue Americans, and the way they see it you can't be a good American and a Jew. So Sam
Goldfish becomes Sam Goldwyn and David Selznick becomes David 0. Selznick -- like anyone's gonna think he's Irish for fuck's sake--

WELLES
What does this have to do with--?

MANK
(dead serious)
Believe you me, they're gonna do anything -- and I mean absolutely anything -- to stop that word from gettin' out.

WELLES
(sharply)
What?! Are they going to kill me? Is that what they're going to do?!
One of the sound technicians turns to Welles:
SOUND TECHNICIAN Sorry, Mr. Welles, I can't really hear
Welles, Mank and Toland quickly decamp to a hallway outside the recording stage...

INT HALLWAY FOLLOWING
They emerge into the hallway. Mank lights a cigar.

MANK
(quietly)
Let me tell you a story, son So this was 1924, right? Hearst was throwing a birthday party for
Thomas Ince, the old movie producer. They were all on the old man's yacht taking a nice jaunt from
Pedro down to San Diego. Real foggy night it was.
This was Hearst, Marion, Ince, Charlie Chaplin,
Louella, the usual gorillas. So Hearst notices
Marion slip off with Chaplin -- she was screwing everyone then -- and the old man goes nuts. Grabs his revolver and starts shooting. Just like Tom Mix, standing there blasting away through the fog. Boom -
- boom -- boom -- and Thomas Ince takes a bullet through the head. So now there's this dead guy lying on the deck. You'll see how this could be quite an embarrassment. So the empire goes into action. Nice and quiet and Ince was cremated lickety-split. No inquest and no police. It was right after this that
Hearst gives Louella her life-time contract. Just to keep her all hush-hush.
A beat as Mank gazes at Welles.
A beat

MANK
If he had known about KANE before you made it, you'd be dead already.

WELLES
(weakly)
It's too late. The movie's made

MANK
They won't let it out. Not Hearst. Not the other studio heads--

WELLES
You wrote the damn thing, Mank Aren't you going to fight for it?!

MANK
(bitterly)
I told you this was going to happen! I told you he was going to come after us! So we took the chance anyway and we lost. That's how it goes, okay? I got my check, kid, and so did you -- and that's what it's all about -- so fuck it and move on.
Welles leans forward in a sudden explosion of anger

WELLES
I WILL NOT MOVE ON! Let them do their worst! These petty tyrants! These monstrous, small men Do they think they can stop us? I Who are they?! Who are they?! THEY ARE . .. ACCOUNTANTS I
Bernard Hermann appears at a doorway from the recording stage.

BERNARD HERMANN
We're ready. You want to hear it?
Welles goes with Hermann into the stage. Toland and Mank stand in silence. Then:

TOLAND
His next picture ... he wants to play Christ.

MANK
Hope he's planning to start with the crucifixion.

76 INT RECORDING STAGE FOLLOWING
Welles sits at the back of the stage, deep in thought
Bernard Hermann raises his baton and prepares to conduct. The opening shots of KANE -- fog shrouded Xanadu -- are projected on the screen.
Hermann conducts and the orchestra plays.
We watch the first images of the film with the brilliant music.
We pull back to reveal we are at

INT SAN SIMEON. SCREENING ROOM NIGHT
Hearst and Marion are sitting in the plush San Simeon screening room, surrounded by a passel of dachshunds. Five or six friends are also spread around the room. Joe Willicombe is also present.

We watch their faces as they watch CITIZEN KANE
During this sequence we hear bits and pieces of KANE as we watch Hearst and Marion react.
We see Marion's initial amusement give way to a forced neutrality.
We see Hearst becoming increasingly uncomfortable, reacting physically, almost writhing, as his soul is laid bare. Then his face grows cold.
Drained.
We see Joe Willicombe, offended.
We see the other guests, horrified and afraid to even so much as glance at Hearst.
Finally, we hear the ending of the movie:

"RAYMOND"
"Throw that junk in, too.
We hear Bernard Hermann's closing music begin to play out
Hearst abruptly stands, the final images of the film washing over his face.

HEARST
Switch it off SWITCH IT OFF
The film suddenly stops and lights come up around the screening room.
Silence No one looks at Hearst.

HEARST
(quietly)
Would everyone please leave
The guests and Joe Willicombe solemnly file out A pause

MARION
Well -- he got us, didn't he?
She stands and goes quickly to pour a drink. A forced laugh

MARION
Nailed us, hub? The crazy old man and his whore.

HEARST
Marion--

MARION
Bought and p-p-paid for. Just like one of his goddamn statues. Well at least in the movie he married her!

HEARST
This picture--

MARION
(deeply)
I am not that woman.

A beat.
I know what I could have been. I know what I gave up to stay with you.

MARION
(pained)
I mean he's even got the goddamn jigsaw puzzles
She dissolves into sobs. He cradles her in the empty screening room
A beat

MARION
Why did he do that to us?

INT SAN SIMEON. ASSEMBLY ROOM NIGHT
Hearst is as we have never seen him before. He is in a titanic rage.
He paces back and forth violently like a caged animal, becoming increasingly manic
and uncontrolled, clenching his fists and barking to
Joe Willicombe:

HEARST
And now of all times -- NOW -- when I am grasping on with my fingernails to live at
all this Orson We lies -- this insect -- this reprehensible insect -- has the nerve TO
CHALLENGE ME! To show my life as some cheap sideshow -- A FREAK SHOW --
A DYING,

IMPOTENT OLD FREAK IN HIS CASTLE!
He smashes a collection of figurines and sends them sailing across the room. Hearst's
rage gives way to a darker passion:

HEARST
(intensely)
Mr. Willicombe -- you have seen me in adversity -- you have seen me take on the unions
and the Congress and the railroads -- and we have risen above -- we have risen above.
And if that dog Welles thinks he can strike at me now -- when he thinks I'm weak when
he thinks I'm vulnerable -- then he does not fully comprehend the man is facing.
WILLICOMBE Mr. Welles can't know anything about the difficulties we're--

HEARST
Get me Louella Parsons, now!
Willicombe picks up a phone and begins dialing as Hearst continues:

HEARST
This upstart -- this puny man -- how does he even dare to imagine he could comprehend
my life and my world when he crawls with the other insects in the sewer -- in the dung
-- when we control every moment of his life from the instant he is born to the instant
we decide that he will die! Does he have no idea of the power that controls him?!

WILLICOMBE
Mr. Hearst, I have Miss Par'
Hearst snatches the phone from Willicombe

HEARST
(on phone)
Miss Parsons, Mr. Hearst. Use the file
He slams down the phone

HEARST
Now get me J. Edgar Hoover
WILLICOMBE It's very late in Washington-

HEARST
Then wake him up!
Willicombe begins to dial

HEARST
(fervently)
That insect thinks he knows me! He thinks he knows my capabilities! When his neck is in my teeth and his blood is in my throat then he will know WILLIAM

RANDOLPH HEARST!
INT MAYER'S OFFICE. MGM DAY
Louis B. Mayor's eyes are blinking behind his glasses
In his glasses we can see vague reflections of a series of grainy photographs showing sex acts and illicit assignations and corpses and mug shots.
We pull back to reveal Mayer flipping through a stack of photos and notes.
Louella sits, smoking and supremely confident, across from him.
Mayer finally closes the file and removes his glasses. He rubs his eyes. He rises unsteadily and goes to a liquor cabinet and pours himself a stiff drink. He gulps it down and then returns to his desk.
A pause and then he finally looks at Louella
A beat
A beat
A beat.
A pause

LOUELLA
So what do we got here, L.B.? We got faggots and commies and junkies. We got movie stars screwing niggers and little girls. We got killers and perverts and whores.

LOUELLA
We got MGM and Warner Brothers and Columbia and
Disney and Fox.

LOUELLA
We got Jews

LOUELLA
We got Hollywood.

MAYER
(quietly)
What do you want?

LOUELLA
Kill CITIZEN KANE.

MAYER
How?

LOUELLA
I don't give a shit.
A beat

LOUELLA
The boss is working on some stuff and I'm working on some stuff. Now I want all you boys working on some stuff. Cause if it looks like this picture's ever gonna come out -- I start running down the street with these pictures like a screaming woman with my throat cut, you follow?

J. EDGAR HOOVER'S OFFICE
DAY
Bulldog-like FBI Director HOOVER sits erect at his desk. Behind him an imposing FBI Seal catches the light.
He presses a button on his intercom.

HOOVER
Agent McCabe, if you please.
His secretary, clean-cut FBI agent McCABE, enters quickly with a note pad. Agent McCabe scribbles as Hoover dictates:

EXT.
HOOVER
Open a new file. Heading: Welles, Orson. Native born. Communist.

HILLS AROUND SAN SIMEON DAY
Marion and Joe Willicombe sit in deck chairs under the blazing sun.
Marion absently pets a dachshund in her lap. Servants stand behind them with lunch and trays of iced tea
They watch Hearst riding a horse in the distance A pause. Then:

MARION
How bad is it?

WILLICOMBE
Miss Davies--

MARION
Come on Joe. How bad is it?
A beat.

WILLICOMBE
It's finished
Hearst gallops up to them. A servant helps him down from his horse. He strides briskly
to Marion and Willicombe as:

HEARST
I've been thinking about the Tribune in Chicago.
The Examiner just can't make any headway.
Circulation is still down. I think we should buy the
Tribune.
Marion glances to Willicombe and then looks at Hearst with great tenderness.

MARION
Sure, Pops. That's a swell idea

INT MANK'S HOUSE. SANTA MONICA DAY
Manks pounding away at a typewriter in his tiny beach house.
He grumbles to himself as he types:

MANK
... and Rita Hayworth says: "You see, he truly was the Son of God" ... big Toland
lighting effect ... blah, blah, blah ...
A knock at the door. Mank answers it. Clean-cut FBI Agent McCabe stands outside. He
flashes his badge.
AGENT McCABE
Mr. Mankiewicz, I'm Special Agent McCabe of the
Federal Bureau of Investigation. Might I have a moment of your time?

MANK
Sure, kid, come in. I'm writing the crucifixion and it's a bitch. Sit down
Agent McCabe sits and snaps open a note pad
AGENT McCABE
I would like to ask you a few questions about Mr.
Welles.

MANK
You guys after Orson too?
AGENT McCABE
Mr. Mankiewicz.

MANK
Shoot
AGENT McCABE
Are you aware of Mr. Welles' Communist affiliations?

MANK
Shit, Orson's no pink. He's everything else under the sun, but he's no pink.
AGENT McCABE
Are you aware of Mr. Welles' Communist affiliations?

MANK
No, I am not
AGENT McCABE
Do you have any knowledge of Communists working within the motion picture industry?
AGENT McCABE
Do you have any knowledge of Communists working within the motion picture industry?

MANK
No
AGENT McCABE
Are you now or have you ever been a member of, or affiliated with, the Communist Party or any of its front organizations in the United States?

MANK
Stop it
AGENT McCABE
Are you now or have you ever been a member of--

MANK
I think you better leave
AGENT McCABE
Are you now or have you--

MANK
(grim)
Get the fuck outta my house.
Agent McCabe snaps his note pad closed and stands.
AGENT McCABE
(crisply)

Thank you for your time, Mr. Mankiewicz. We'll be in touch.
Agent McCabe leaves

MANK
(calling after him)
Don't bother, you low-life prick
Mank slams the door
He stands for a moment, pale, and then goes to the kitchen and pours himself a stiff drink.

INT SAN SIMEON, ASSEMBLY ROOM DAY
Marion is pouring a drink as well. She quickly fills a glass of Scotch and then begins striding back and forth across the Assembly Room.
Hearst sits quietly at one of the jigsaw puzzles He occasionally and absently puts a piece in place.
She has clearly been at him for some time

MARION
Then you explain it to me?!

HEARST
There's nothing to explain

MARION
A million dollars a year on art and st-st-statues and there's nothing to explain?!

HEARST
I will not defend my life to you--

MARION
I'm not asking you to defend anything. But we're in a pickle and we gotta talk about it.

HEARST
We are in no "pickle" -- as you would euphemistically have it.

MARION
You gotta wake up now. Pops.

HEARST
There is nothing to discuss-

MARION
You don't have any money left, okay?! That's the truth. I don't wanna say it, nobody else will say it, but it's the truth. You spent it all. You can't buy the Tribune in Chicago -- you can't buy ^ g-g- goddamn thing. Now you better face up to it--

HEARST
You are being typically theatrical, Marion. I need the Tribune to--

MARION
You don't need it! That's the problem you always think you need everything--
Marion spins to a medieval arras cloth hanging from one wall.

MARION
That -- did you need that? How much did that cost?

HEARST
It's 12th Century. From Deauville -- in France.

MARION
I know where Deauville is for C-C-Christ's sake.

HEARST
You needn't use that language with me

MARION
Did you need it? Did you need any of it?

HEARST
I wanted it

MARION
There's a different between want and

HEARST
(tightly)
Not for me.

MARION
(frustrated)
But why? Just so you can show it all off -- just so everyone can see what a b-b-big man
you are?!
He stands quickly

HEARST
(angrily)
That's right. You've captured me exactly.
Goodnight.

MARION
You will not walk out on me

HEARST
You are repellant when you drink.

MARION
Tough shit. We need to t-t-talk about this--

HEARST
You are slovenly and unattractive and I won't (he mercilessly mimics her) t-t-t-tolerate it.
A cold beat
A pause.

MARION
Fuck you, Mr. Kane.

HEARST
(darkly)
I will not have this in my home.

MARION
I just want to understand--

HEARST
(suddenly)
No, you don't. You want to condemn me, like everyone else. You want to point to the pathetic, old man grown lunatic with his spending -- trapped in his ridiculous

HEARST (CONT.) castle -- still fighting old battles he will never win with Pulitzer and Roosevelt and Hollywood--

MARION
I don't want you to--

HEARST
There is nothing to understand but this: I am a man who could have been great, but was not.
He leaves

INT SAN SIMEOM. MARION'S BEDROOM DAY
A silent scene as we see Marion rummaging through some drawers in her vanity table. A suitcase can be seen on the bed behind her.
She removes various jewelry cases and pours an astounding array of gems into a black leather pouch.

INT. ELIZABETH ARDEN SALON. BEVERLY HILLS DAY
Marion sits with Carole Lombard in a secluded section of the luxurious salon.

A quiet scene.

MARION
When I met him I was just 20. And he was 55. I saw the gold ring and just grabbed on.
And he was going to make me a star.

CAROLE LOMBARD
And he did.
A beat.

MARION
When I was making movies I kept begging him to let me do comedies. Silly stuff, you
know. But Pops doesn't get comedy too well so he kept putting me in all those godawful
p-p-period dramas.
Carole Lombard smiles.

MARION
I did my best but, well, you know me

CAROLE LOMBARD
Sure

MARION
Thing that bothers me now, though, looking back is that I really think I could have been
something ... special.

CAROLE LOMBARD
Thinking like that is only gonna drive you nuts You were a great star and you had a
good run. That oughta be enough.

MARION
Yeah. But all of a sudden it's not

MARION
You know this CITIZEN KANE picture? About Pops and everything?

CAROLE LOMBARD
Uh-huh

MARION
The character that's supposed to be me, Susan
Alexander--

CAROLE LOMBARD
Marion, everyone knows you're not like that--

MARION
But I am That's the killer, honey.
This little girl comes from nowhere and gets discovered by this guy.
And maybe she has some real talent way deep down. But he pays the bills and he makes
the decisions. And somewhere along the way ... she gets lost.

MARION
It's hell when you gotta look back and say, goddamn, what I could have been.

JEWELRY STORE. BEVERLY HILLS
Marion enters a posh Beverly Hills jewelry shop. She is wearing sunglasses.
She nervously goes to the counter and the SHOP OWNER glides to her. For
Marion, the entire experience is humiliating. This results in her stutter becoming
increasingly more pronounced.

SHOP OWNER
May I help you?

MARION
I, um, need an estimate on some jewelry I might wish to sell. But d-d-discretion is very
important to me b-b-because I don't want anyone t-t-to, um, know that--

SHOP OWNER
Excuse me, I hope this isn't rude, but aren't you
Marion Davies?

MARION
Yes.

SHOP OWNER
Well, this is a great pleasure. Miss Davies! I just saw that ENCHANTMENT is playing
at a the Tivoli, the revival house in Santa Monica. That was a fine picture!

MARION
Thank you-

SHOP OWNER
Not one of them today has what you had, Miss
Davies. Not one of them.

MARION
Thank you -- b-b-but I'd really like t-t-to--

SHOP OWNER
Of course, of course. How can we be of service?

MARION
As I said I have some j-j-j-j- (she simply can't get the word out) that I might wish t-t-to
sell and
I wanted an estimate--

SHOP OWNER
Surely My pleasure, Miss Davies..
Marion removes the leather pouch from her purse and pours a stunning collection of
jewelry on a black felt tablet on the counter.

SHOP OWNER
(awed)
My Lord. . .
Marion removes her sunglasses and looks at him. Her eyes are red.

MARION
How much for the lot?

EXT RKO LOT DAY
Welles is pursuing Schaefer as they stride through the bustling RKO backlot.

SCHAEFER
What do you want me to do, Orson? Radio City won't premiere the picture. Louella
threatened them with some bullshit about

WELLES
Then find another theater

SCHAEFER
You don't think I've tried? No one is willing to open the picture

WELLES
Then we'll open it in Detroit or Dallas or
Kalamazoo for God's sake! We'll show it in goddamn circus tents and--!
Schaefer stops.

SCHAEFER
Listen to me. The press ban is killing us and the distributors won't book it. And
meantime I'm dealing with the stockholders in New York who are scared shitless -- and
I'm this far from getting fired myself -- and you don't have a friend in the world but me
right now. So you have got to trust that I'll do what I can to--

WELLES
(desperately)
"Do what you can"?! That's not good enough I

SCHAEFER
Well it' s all you've got !

WELLES
(suddenly)
You're with them, aren't you? You're going to bury my movie. They bought you!

SCHAEFER
(turning away)
For Christ's sake, shut up--

WELLES
Why don't you just have the guts to admit it

SCHAEFER
(spinning on him)
How dare you talk to me like that! Do you think I'm like all the rest of those pirates?! Like Mayer and
Warner? Is that what you think--?!

WELLES
It's just that my movie is so-

SCHAEFER
(savagely)
"Your movie" -- I am so sick of that! It's your movie -- but it's his life! Did you ever think about that?! Did you ever think about that old man and
Marion having to watch as you tore them apart?!

WELLES
I didn't--

SCHAEFER
Do you every think for one second that you might have some responsibility for what you're doing?! For cutting and slashing everything in your way so you can have your goddamn movie?!

WELLES
That soulless monster gets no tears from me.

SCHAEFER
Who the fuck are you trying to kid? You are that soulless monster.
Schaefer turns and stomps away Welles stands, lost for a moment in the dream factory
In a bit of a daze, Welles slowly begins walking through the backlot. A bustle of loud activity in a corner of the lot draws his attention.

A bulldozer and a dozen workmen are busy tearing down the facade of a large white mansion. They strip the wood off and toss it into an incinerator.
Welles sees Schaefer standing before all this activity, deep in thought.
Welles goes to him and they stand together in silence for a moment as they watch the house being razed.

SCHAEFER
Recognize
Welles shakes his head

SCHAEFER
It's Tara. From GONE WITH THE WIND
Pause as they watch Scarlett O'Hara's dream mansion being torn apart.

WELLES
It's ... sad
A beat.

SCHAEFER
Not really. It's only a set, after all Just lumber.

.

SCHAEFER
(quietly)
You know, we make all these pictures, we turn em out one after another, without thinking most of the time. Just like making toasters or Packards or toothpaste. But then sometimes ... something amazing happens and you get a GONE WITH THE WIND.
Or a CITIZEN KANE

SCHAEFER (CONT.)
And no one can ever take that away from you.
They gaze at the destruction of Tara as we hear:

RADIO ANNOUNCER (VOICE OVER)
... and in financial news, rumors continue to swirl around the head of publishing baron William Randolph
Hearst. . .

INT SAN SIMEON. ROMAN POOL NIGHT
Hearst sits in a wicker chair by the shimmering in-door Roman Pool. But for Hearst and the single chair, the pool is deserted and has no other furniture.
Hearst is staring at the gold and blue mosaic of tiles reflected in the water.
As we hear:

RADIO ANNOUNCER (VOICE OVER, CONT.)

... Sources report that the Hearst Empire is facing some rocky times ahead as the press lord is facing mounting debts and shrinking revenues due to over expansion and fiscal mismanagement that have resulted in...

The radio voice fades to silence.

The silence continues but for the haunting echo of a lion roaring in the distance. Then Hearst hears the sound of footsteps echoing on the tile. He looks up. It is Marion. She walks around the pool to him.

Without a word she hands him a check.

It is made out to William Randolph Hearst in the amount of one million dollars and is signed Marion Davies.

A long pause. He looks up at her, profoundly moved.

MARION

I started out as a gold-digger, ya know But goddamn if I didn't fall in love with the guy.

EXT MAYER'S ESTATE DAY

A row of six shining limousines are lined up in front of Mayor's enormous house. The chauffeurs stand together and chat.

EXT. MAYER'S ESTATE. BACKYARD

Mayer sits in the glorious back garden of his house. Six other men are gathered around him.

Mayer nods his head to each as we pan around the faces

MAYER

Mr. Zanuck ... Mr. Warner ... Mr. Cohn Mr. Disney
.. . Mr. Goldwyn ...Mr. Selznick.
A beat.
Thank you all for coming. You got my memo. What do we do?
A beat

JACK WARNER

He's a fucking punk, why does Hearst give a shit?

MAYER

It's enough that he does

SAM GOLDWYN

Would Louella really do it?

MAYER

In a New York minute

DAVID 0. SELZNICK

I say to hell with Louella and to hell with Hearst!
Bring 'em on. We can take em.

HARRY COHN
We all didn't make GONE WITH THE WIND, ya know.
Some of us gotta look at this checkbook-wise.

MAYER
Who isn't hurting already? All this Jew talk and these Communist rumors. Look, he's boycotting RKO ads right now -- but how long before he takes on
Warners or Fox or Columbia?

HARRY COHN
Goddamn right.
A beat.

MAYER
And if Hearst goes public with all this filthy private lives stuff, Hollywood's sunk. He's got us nailed. Dates. Times. Photographs for God's sake.

WALT DISNEY
I don't mean to be funny, but what could he have on
Mickey Mouse?

MAYER
He's got you so tied in with J. Edgar Hoover and
America First that you might as well put on a brown shirt and kiss those happy little kiddies so-long.

DAVID 0. SELZNICK
(suddenly)
Have any of you actually seen the movie?
A beat.

DAVID 0. SELZNICK
I have. It's probably the greatest motion picture ever made. Nothing's going to be the same after this. With this one movie he's changed the way we see--

JACK WARNER
Who the fuck cares?

DAVID 0. SELZNICK
I do. And so should all of you--

JACK WARNER
Get off the soapbox--
Selznick stands.

DAVID 0. SELZNICK
I want no part of this. We should be marching into
George Schaefer's office and standing with him. He's one of us!

MAYER
David-

DAVID 0. SELZNICK
If I ever got into trouble I'd like to think that you all would be with me -- not planning
to stab me in the back like a bunch of ... a bunch of ... producers!
He storms off

JACK WARNER
(to Mayer)
Your son-in-law meshuaena.
A pause.
Laughter
A pause.

DISNEY
(nervously)
He's got me and Hoover?

JACK WARNER
Relax, Walt, at least he don't have you screwing
Snow White. I got fucking Errol Flynn on my payroll!

SAM GOLDWYN
(to Mayer)
You're a smart man, L.B. I suspect you would not have called us here without a plan.
Give over.

MAYER
We will buy the movie and we will destroy it.

MAYER
We will assemble a fund between us -- privately,
'not studio money -- we will assemble this fund and we will go to George Schaefer and
we will buy the negative and every print of CITIZEN KANE and we will burn them.
A long pause

MAYER
If I do not hear an objection to this agenda in the next five seconds I will assume the
motion has carried.
Five seconds tick by as we focus on the titans of Hollywood

MAYER
Very well, my associates will be in touch to arrange payment. Thank you for your time.

INT RECORDING STAGE DAY
KANE composer Bernard Hermann again stands before the orchestra, his arm poised, waiting to begin conducting. He is about to record some new music for the deep-focus Thatcher/Bernstein/Kane scene from CITIZEN

KANE.
Welles sits nearby, supervising everything. Welles nods and on a movie screen the scene from KANE begins and Hermann starts conducting. The orchestra plays.
The music carries into and gradually fades during.

INT SAN SIMEON. ASSEMBLY ROOM DAY
In a scene eerily reminiscent of the Thatcher/Bernstein/Kane scene,
Marion sits in the extreme foreground, a man we do not know sits at middle distance at a desk and Hearst stands far away.
Hearst has his back to them and stares out a window.
The new man is MR. LEWIS, a tight banker from New York, 50's.
He looks over a thick legal document on the desk as he speaks:
LEWIS You will retain some editorial control over the remaining newspapers but the actual ownership will go to the Conservation
Committee and the banks. We will be immediately closing 12 of the papers and the wire services. And we will be liquidating other assets as soon as possible. Most of the land in Mexico as well as your collection of art and antiquities--

MARION
(quietly)
Mr. Hearst spent his life collecting that art.

LEWIS
(ignoring her)
We've been in touch with Gimbels in New York and they've agreed to hold a special sale. They're giving over an entire floor for the merchandise.
You'll have to go there in person to sign the bill of sale, by the way.

HEARST
(softly, not turning)
I'll have to sell the animals.

LEWIS
And we don't know whether we'll be able to retain the castle. The land has some capital and we might keep it on as an investment. Maybe break it up into smaller units for housing.
A long pause Hearst finally turns and walks to them.

HEARST
(to Lewis)
When will it come out? When will the public know?

LEWIS
We can't keep it a secret, sir. Once we announce the Gimbels sale and start liquidating
the assets.

MARION
(pained)
This is your whole life. Pops. Don't do it. We'll find another way..
A long beat as he looks at her. Then he quickly signs the document on the desk. He puts
down the pen and leaves the room without a word

INT SAN SIMEON. STAIRWAY NIGHT
Marion sits nestled on a sweeping marble stairway Weeping

INT NIGHTCLUB. HOLLYWOOD NIGHT
A swank benefit dinner is in progress A band plays
A banner hangs over the nightclub stage: CHILDREN'S MILK FUND BENEFIT,

1940
We float through the elegant crowd and spy Louis B. Mayer and Louella;
Clark Gable and Carole Lombard; all manner of movie stars and power brokers.
We also spy Schaefer sitting with Mank and Toland and a few other men and women.
The evening's EMCEE takes the stage

EMCEE
Next up we have a real treat. It's Orson Welles.
Now, during the rehearsal for the benefit tonight
Orson banished everyone from the club so he could proceed in utmost secrecy. But you
all know how
Orson is!
Laughter from the crowd

EMCEE
So, lets give a big round of applause for Mr. Orson
Welles and Miss Rita Hayworth.
Polite applause as Welles bounds to the stage with RITA HAYWORTH and the band
begins to play a buoyant tune.
Schaefer practically drops his fork
Welles is dressed in a padded costume and made up in a way that can suggest no one
but William Randolph Hearst. Rita Hayworth is dressed in a manner mightily like
Marion Davies.
Louella glances to Mayer, daggers. Some knowing laughter from the audience.
Particularly Mank

A line of chorus girls hoof on and join Welles and Rita Hayworth as a row of harsh footlights snap on, giving the scene a resemblance to the
"Charlie Kane" dance in CITIZEN KANE.
And Welles launches into a jaunty song and dance version of
"DISGUSTINGLY RICH" an almost unknown Rodgers and Hart song;'. Welles has wickedly changed some of the lines. '

WELLES
"I'll buy everything I wear at Saks. I'll print gossip and I'll call it facts

RITA HAYWORTH
"Swear like a trooper, Live in a stupor--

WELLES AND RITA HAYWORTH
"Just disgustingly rich!

WELLES
"I'll make money and I'll make it quick, Starting little wars I think are slick. Smother her in sables, Like Betty Grable's-- Just disgustingly rich. "I'll build a castle, That'll cost a passel.
And as a resident, I will pan the president I'll aspire, Higher and Higher. "I'll get married and
I'll buy a girl, So darn pretty that your head will swirl

RITA HAYWORTH
"Swimming in highballs-- Stewed to the eyeballs--

WELLES AND RITA HAYWORTH
"Just disgustingly rich!
Welles, Rita Hayworth and the chorines do a nifty soft-shoe turn as
Schaefer turns to Mank:

SCHAEFER
(seriously)
He truly doesn't care if he ever works again.

MANK
Yeah, ain't it swell?
Welles and Rita Hayworth conclude their little dance break and Welles resumes the song:

WELLES
"Ev'ry summer I will sail the sea, On my little yacht the Normandie, Pet my little dachshund friends, Kiss Louella's big rear end, Just disgustingly rich.
About here Louella storms out.
"I'll eat salmon, I'll play backgammon. Turn breakfast into brunch,

I'll take Thomas Ince to lunch I'll aspire, Higher and Higher.
About here Louis B Mayer and a few others storm out.

RITA HAYWORTH
"He'll be photographed with Myrna Loy, Just to prove he is a glamour boy.

WELLES
"Perfumed and scented, Slightly demented-- Just disgustingly rich

RITA HAYWORTH
"I'll get my capers, Into his papers. Hoping his folly would Lead me out to Hollywood. I'll aspire,
Higher and higher.
About here Schaefer buries his face in his hands

WELLES AND RITA HAYWORTH
"In the funnies and the valentines, We'll be pictured drinking Ballantine's. Dopey and screwy,
Voting for Dewey. Just disgustingly-- Too, too disgustingly-- Riiiiich! "
Welles and Rita Hayworth conclude the number with a big flourish.
Some applause
Mank stands and applauds loudly. Laughing. Welles bows solemnly to Mank

EXT NIGHTCLUB FOLLOWING
Later that night, Welles is about to climb into his limousine outside the nightclub with Rita Hayworth when Schaefer suddenly appears and grabs his lapel.

WELLES
(happily)
George- -!
Without a word, Schaefer pulls Welles roughly into an alley beside the nightclub. He slams Welles into the alley wall.

SCHAEFER
(brutally)
This isn' t some kinda fucking game! You know how many people RKO employs?! You know how many people depend on what we do for a living?!

WELLES
I really think you're

SCHAEFER
You wanna commit suicide, fine! You got some death- wish, fine! But you will not drag this company down with you!

WELLES

It was a -joke, George
Schaefer slaps Welles firmly across the face. Welles is stunned.

SCHAEFER
There are no jokes! There are people making a living. There is food on the table!
Schaefer glares at him and then rages off
Welles straightens his suit and then, with a shaking hand, reaches for a cigar. He tries
to laugh, but cannot.

INT SCHAEFER'S OFFICE. RKO DAY
Schaefer sits at his desk, absolutely dazed. Speechless
B. Mayer sits across from him.

SCHAEFER
Where did this money come from? beat

MAYER
It came.

MAYER
800,000 dollars fully covers the production budget and a little more. Hell, George, you
even make a profit on the deal.

SCHAEFER
Very generous

MAYER
And we gotta be clear here. I need the negative and every existing print.

SCHAEFER
To do what?

MAYER
That's for me to decide.

SCHAEFER
You're going to destroy it

MAYER
No, maybe put it on the shelf until the old man kicks it.

SCHAEFER
You're lying to me.

MAYER
We already made the same offer to the stockholders.

Schaefer is stunned.

SCHAEFER
You talked to New York?

MAYER
Yes

SCHAEFER
You talked to Mr. Swanbeck?
Pause.

MAYER
Yes

SCHAEFER
Get out

MAYER
You're bettin' on an inside straight this time.
You'll never pull it off.

SCHAEFER
Get out.
Mayer stands and smiles

MAYER
This picture, George, it'll just break your heart.
Mayer goes. Schaefer sits, smelling defeat.
We linger on Schaefer as a haunting echo of "I CAN'T GET STARTED" is heard. . .

INT/EXT SAN SIMEON NIGHT
We float through the estate as we hear the ghostly strains of Bunny
Berigan's recording of "I CAN'T GET STARTED."
It is a sad journey.
By this time many of the ornate antiquities have been removed from the castle and it
resembles Welles' stark and dreary Xanadu all the more.

BUNNY BERIGAN
"I've flown around the world in a plane, I've settled revolutions in Spain, And the North
Pole I have charted, Still I can't get started with you...
We float past the private zoo, now empty, the cages hanging open. We move past the
tennis courts, empty.

BUNNY BERIGAN

"On the golf course I'm under par, Metro Goldwyn has asked me to star, I've got a house, a show place, Still I can't get no place with you.
We float into the castle itself and through the stripped- down
Screening Room and the Assembly Room and the Great Dining Hall.
All are mere shadows of their past glory.

BUNNY BERIGAN
"Cause you're so supreme, Lyrics I write of you, I dream, dream day and night of you
And I scheme just for the sight of you, Baby, what good does it do...?
We finally float into the ballroom
A record of "I CAN'T GET STARTED" spins forlornly on a turntable.
And Marion and Hearst are having a quiet, poignant dance together in the middle of the empty ballroom.

BUNNY BERIGAN
"I've been consulted by Franklin D. Greta Garbo has had me to tea, Still I'm broken hearted Cause I can't get started with you.
They finally stop dancing and stand swaying gently. Then they stop swaying.

HEARST
(gently)
Ah, Miss Davies, the times we have seen
She holds him closely as "I CAN'T GET STARTED" concludes

INT CHASEN'S RESTAURANT. PRIVATE ROOM DAY
Welles has booked a private room at Chasen's. A long banquet table contains cans of sterno heating various dishes.
Large photographs of the American West and renderings from THE LIFE OF
CHRIST are scattered around other tables.
Welles wanders around the renderings with Gregg Toland and Mank. Welles carries a plate of food and consumes as:

TOLAND
See, this is the Great Salt Lake -- we do the baptism here.

MANK
Great scene where John the Baptist pulls your head out of the water and says, "Look up, and behold your destiny"

WELLES
Is that from one of the Gospels?

MANK
Kinda.
Schaefer enters.

WELLES
George! Enter And Behold
Schaefer blinks at the massive photos and renderings.

WELLES
You're not still mad at me, I hope

SCHAEFER
No, we're jake. But listen-

WELLES
Look, not a single scene shot in the studio! We've found natural locations for the whole
story--

SCHAEFER
Hold on a sec. I got news. We finally found somewhere to premiere KANE but--

WELLES
I told you! Where? Grauman's? El Capitan? Or did
Radio City come crawling back?

SCHAEFER
The Palace in New York. But Orson there's something else.
Welles stops eating

SCHAEFER
I think you better sit down

WELLES
(evenly)
I don't want to sit
Beat.

SCHAEFER
The bosses -- the other studios -- they want to buy the film and destroy it.
Absolute silence
Pause

SCHAEFER
They came to me with an offer. 800,000 for the negative and all the prints.

SCHAEFER
And they went to the stockholders in New York.

MANK
(quietly)

Oh God.

SCHAEFER
I been talking to Swanbeck in New York and...
Orson, I think they're gonna take it A long pause as
Welles looks at Schaefer
Welles suddenly FLINGS his plate of food in Schaefer's direction as he

ROARS:
WELLES
**YOU STUPID, LITTLE MAN! HOW COULD YOU HAVE LET THIS
HAPPEN?! I GAVE YOU MY SOUL AND NOW YOU'RE GOING TO
SELL IT!?**
MANK
This ain't George's doing--!
Welles- rampages around the room

WELLES
**I PUT MY LIFE INTO THAT PICTURE -- EVERYTHING I'VE
BEEN -- EVERYTHING I COULD BE---IT'S CITIZEN KANE! -
- IT'S ALL CITIZEN KANE!**
And in a screaming, bellowing fury, Welles tears apart the room.
In a scene sharply reminiscent of Kane destroying Susan's bedroom,
Welles rampages around the room, upsetting tables and smashing everything in reach.
Welles finally grabs a flaming can of sterno and flings it at Schaefer,
Schaefer knocks it away.
Then Welles stands in spent exhaustion, panting. One of his hands is bleeding.
He looks at Schaefer. A pause. Then:

WELLES
Let ...me ...talk to them. . .
New York ... The stockholders
Give me one chance. And then you will never have to see me again.

INT. GIMBELS NEW YORK DAY
The entire two-acre fifth floor of Gimbels is in chaos
A large banner is suspended at one end of the floor; "The Hearst
Collection." It is the first day of the sale and it is mobbed.
Hearst and Marion, alone in a crowd, walk wordlessly through the mayhem.
Everywhere around them hundreds of eager customers strike like hawks, snatching up
useless junk and treasured antiques.
We see bits and pieces of San Simeon in the jumble
They pass a man and his wife, holding up Marion's -BLESS THIS CASTLE" sampler:

MAN
Old man Hearst owned this and I'm getting it for two bits I

Hearst and Marion continue to walk, finally arriving at the section containing the true, expensive treasures.

Hearst watches as customers pick up and fondle his life.

He glances at a framed front page of the San Francisco Examiner. The date is March 4, 1887. In a large box on the page is: "IT IS THE ROLE

OF THE PRESS TO COMFORT THE AFFLICTED AND AFFLICT THE COMFORTABLE.
WILLIAM RANDOLPH HEARST. PUBLISHER."
HEARST
I can't sell this. How much are they asking?

MARION
(gently)
Pops ... let it go. Just ... let it go
He looks at her. A long moment. He tenderly touches her face.
Then:

HEARST
Yes, I think I shall.
He takes her hand and leads her away as we pull up and take in the entire fifth floor.
It is a stunning KANE-like image of rows and rows of merchandise piled high. Of junk and jewels. Of Charles Foster Kane and William Randolph
Hearst.

INT HOTEL ROOM. NEW YORK NIGHT
Welles sits brooding in his hotel room. His invincible energy appears gone.
He is deep in thought, listlessly shuffling and reshuffling a deck of cards in one hand.
He aimlessly shuffles through the cards and plucks one out.

WELLES
Six of spades
He glances at the card. It is the nine of hearts.
He shuffles through the cards again and pulls out another card.

WELLES
Six of spades
He looks at the card. It is the two of clubs.
His attention is now fully on the cards. He shuffles them dramatically and snatches out a card. He looks at it and then tosses it away. He shuffles again, working the trick, again it fails. He tosses another card away. He continues, ;' more quickly, to attempt the trick. It fails again. And ' again.
With a frightened moan Welles flings the entire deck away from him and bolts out of the room...

EXT HOTEL ROOFTOP NIGHT

Welles emerges from a stairway on the roof of his hotel.

He marches to the edge of the roof and leans against a railing, gasping for air.

Everywhere below him the shimmering lights of Manhattan twinkle and flash; cabs and neon and noise. The night sky above him is filled with stars.

He looks away from the city and up to the stars -- they captivate him fully. He stares and stares at the impossible chaos of beautiful lights.

A long moment as Welles gazes at the stars. The city below and the noise seem to disappear and Welles stands, safe and at peace under the silent dome of stars.

The stars are reflected in his huge, dark eyes

Magically, the stars in his eyes give way to the vague shapes of men sitting around a table.

Welles looks at the men.

WELLES

Today.

We pull back to see we are at

INT RKO BOARD ROOM. NEW YORK DAY

Welles stands at the head of a long conference table. Title: APRIL 6,

1941

Around the table are gathered a group of stern businessmen Schaefer is also present.

Welles looks at the men. And he speaks. For once, his usual overwrought, theatrical tones are gone.

He speaks simply.

WELLES

Today a man from Germany invaded Greece. He has already swallowed Poland and Denmark and Norway and

Belgium. He is bombing London as I speak. Everywhere this man goes he crushes the life and the freedom of his subjects. He sews yellow stars onto their lapels. He takes their voices.

In this country we still have our voices. And we can sing with them.

And we can argue with them. And we can be heard. Because we are ...for the moment ...free. No one can tell us what to say or how to say it, can they? We have no brown shirt thugs here ruling our lives, do we? No one can take our voices, can they? Because we are free.

I am one voice and that is all. My picture is one voice. Men are dying in Europe now -- and Americans soon will be -- so that we can surmount the tyrants and the dictators. Will you send a message across this country that one man can take away our voices?

So ... who is Mr. Hearst and who is Mr. Welles? Mr. Hearst built a palace of brick and mortar and starting little wars and corpses piled high. I built a palace of illusion. My castle Xanadu is a matte painting and camera trick. It's nothing but ...a dream.

Today you have a chance to let the dream triumph. For once.

He gazes at them and then slowly walks out of the room

INT LONG HALLWAY. NEW YORK DAY
Welles sits quietly on a bench in a long hallway in a tall building.
Schaefer emerges from an office and goes to him. He sits next to him.

SCHAEFER
We open on May 1st.
Welles slowly nods.

SCHAEFER
Orson, what you said in there. Did you mean it?
Welles looks at him.

WELLES
Does it matter? They believed it
He stands and begins walking away.

SCHAEFER
Orson.
Welles stops, not turning.

SCHAEFER
Yes. It matters.
Welles continues down the hall

INT HOTEL. NEW YORK NIGHT
Title: APRIL 30, 1941 Welles is rushing to catch an elevator as the doors close
He nips in at the last minute and punches his button. He turns.
The elevator is deserted but for one other person: William Randolph
Hearst.
Welles and Hearst recognize each other instantly. As the elevator ascends the two men
look at each other.
A very long pause as we watch their faces -- the young man and the old man -- both
men of mad grandeur and malevolent passion and stunning inspiration -- both men of
incalculable achievement and measureless poignancy.
Finally:

WELLES
Mr. Hearst, we've met once before, my name is Orson
Welles and I've got a movie opening tomorrow night at the Palace. I would be pleased
to get you tickets.
A pause as Hearst regards Welles.
Then Hearst carefully reaches over and presses the stop button on the elevator. The
elevator stops.
An exceedingly quiet exchange:
A beat.
A pause.

HEARST

I wonder. Do you have any idea what you have done?

WELLES

Do you?

HEARST

Intimately. For every sin you have placed on my head I could give you a hundred others. I have been swimming in blood my entire life. But I retain a belief, perhaps you will think it old fashioned, undoubtedly you will, but I believe that private lives should not be public property.

WELLES

Elegant words, sir, when you have made your name and your fortune on slander and innuendo and gossip.
In your papers you taught the world how to look under every rock. I learned at the knee of the master.

HEARST

So where does that leave us, Mr. Welles? What kind of sad future are we two making? A future where men will do anything to sell their newspapers and their movies? A future where no price is too high for fame and power? When we will all scratch each other to pieces just to be heard?
Can you truly envision such ... horror.
Hearst presses the stop button again and the elevator begins to move.
The doors opens on Hearst's floor and he leaves the elevator.
The doors are about to shut on Welles when he leans forward; and roars:

WELLES
CHARLES FOSTER KANE WOULD HAVE ACCEPTED I
The doors shut on Welles and we remain with Hearst as he slowly walks down the long hotel hallway.
He walks with dignity.

EXT PALACE THEATER. NEW YORK NIGHT
It is the premiere of CITIZEN KANE, at last.
The Palace Theater swarms with tuxedos and dress gowns as the elite of
New York and Hollywood descend from limousines and slowly parade into the packed lobby.
On the Palace marquee "ORSON WELLES" is spelled out in enormous six foot tall electric letters. Below that is "CITIZEN KANE" also in electric letters. Above the marquee is a series of towering, flashing neon Charles Foster Kanes and the words "IT'S TERRIFIC."
Title; MAY 1, 1941
We float down and enter the crowded lobby with the patrons...

INT PALACE THEATER. LOBBY FOLLOWING
We swirl with the throng of patrons in the lobby as they file into the theater and finally find Welles and Schaefer huddled together nervously in a corner of the lobby.
They are studiously ignored and snubbed by all the movie people filtering past.

SCHAEFER
They're cutting us dead, every goddamn one.
They are ignored by a few more people
Beat

WELLES
It's my birthday this week. I'll be 26.

SCHAEFER
Happy birthday.
Mank fights through the crowd

MANK
Monstro! Ran into Walter Winchell outside He wants to play Herod in the picture. Hiya, George.

SCHAEFER
Herman.

MANK
(lighting a cigar)
So ain't this just the bee's knees? The high muckey-mucks dolled up all Aztec-like for the human sacrifice.

WELLES
You gonna watch?

MANK
Hell, I know how it ends.
(He calls to a passing stranger)
Hey, Rosebud's the sled!

WELLES
Mank!

MANK
Face it, Orson, they're gonna hate it. I told you, not enough closeups and too many scenes with a bunch of New York actors.

SCHAEFER

(pained)
Oh God. . .

WELLES
Relax, George. It's gonna go great. Trust me. Have
I ever lied to you?
Schaefer looks at him for a moment

SCHAEFER
You know something, Orson, you haven't done anything but lie to me from the moment
we met. But, ya know, I'd do it again in a second.

WELLES
It was fun, wasn't it?

SCHAEFER
(quietly)
It was the best, kid

WELLES
So, on to the Life Of Christ!

SCHAEFER
Without me. I'm afraid. I got the axe this morning.

MANK
Shit

WELLES
George...

SCHAEFER
Forget it. Cause you know something..
When I'm an old coot playing dominoes down in Miami Beach fifty years from now,
I'll say, "Hey, you kids ever heard of a guy named Randolph
Hearst?" And they'll say, "Nope. Never heard of him." And then I'll say, "Hey, you ever
heard of a picture called CITIZEN KANE?" And they will have. That's enough for me.
Pats Welles arm and goes into the theater

WELLES
(softly)
What have I done?

MANK
Aw, cheer up, George'll probably be running Fox by the morning. Let's get a drink.
Mank pulls at Welles' arm.

WELLES
But the picture...
Mank stops and looks at him deeply.

MANK
(quietly)
Kid, you know how it ends too. It ends sadly.
He pulls Welles away from the theater and down the street.

INT. PALACE THEATER - NIGHT
We watch the faces
In the flickering blue light we watch the audience as we hear Bernard
Hermann's evocative and haunting opening music to CITIZEN KANE.
We slowly move across a sea of faces as the music plays. For everyone, especially the movie people, what they are seeing is a revelation and a revolution. It is a whole new way of seeing the world.
We see their amazement as they are mesmerized -- and their confusion as they are challenged.
And we see George Schacfcr, quietly proud.
Bernard Hermann's opening music continues to play until we finally hear;

"KANE"
"Rosebud...
And the world of movies is forever changed

INT DESERTED BAR. NEW YORK NIGHT
Welles and Mank are sitting in a rundown, deserted bar

WELLES
You know, all this nightmare we went through with Hearst. The whole thing... And in the end, probably no one will ever remember the picture anyway.

MANK
Yeah, you're probably right.
A beat. Mank takes a drink.

MANK
I'll tell ya something, kid. When you make your masterpiece at 26 it's a bitch. I mean. where do you go from here?
A long pause
Then Welles speaks, softly.

WELLES
Will burn. Burn up. Burn out. But oh, what a flame
He looks at Mank and toasts.

WELLES
Cheers.
And Orson Welles smiles. Indomitable.

THE END.